MW01037731

THE BOXCAR CHILDREN

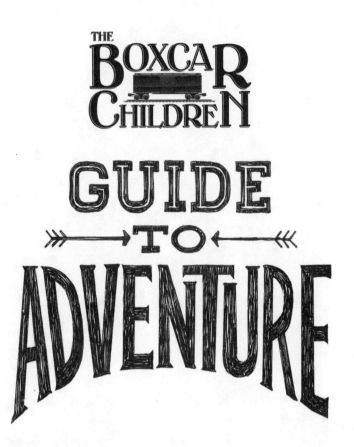

GUIDE
»»»→TO←«««
ADVENTURE

A How-To for Mystery Solving,
Make-It-Yourself Projects, and More

THE BOXCAR CHILDREN

GUIDE ⇥TO⇤ ADVENTURE

A How-To for Mystery Solving, Make-It-Yourself Projects, and More

created by
GERTRUDE CHANDLER WARNER

Albert Whitman & Company
Chicago, Illinois

Library of Congress Cataloging-in-Publication data
is on file with the publisher.

Published in 2014 by Albert Whitman & Company
©2014 Albert Whitman & Company
ISBN 978-0-8075-0905-0
Printed in the United States of America.
10 9 8 7 6 5 4 3 2 1 LB 20 19 18 17 16 15 14

Cover design by Jenna Stempel
Illustrations on pp.1, 2, 3, 7, 8, 10, 11, 12, 42, 46, 52, 54, 63, 69, 71, 81,
82, 93, 94, 98, 110, 113, 116, 122, 124, 127, 128, 136, 144
by Anthony Van Arsdale
Illustrations on pp.vi, 4, 24, 26, 74, 76 by Tim Jessell

For more information about Albert Whitman & Company,
visit our web site at www.albertwhitman.com.

Contents

Introduction

Jessie Alden loves to be organized. When she and her siblings—Henry, Benny, and Violet—found an old boxcar in the woods, Jessie's knack for organizing helped turn the place into a home. As their adventures have continued, Jessie writes things down in a notebook so she can remember them later. Now she has enough lists, ideas, and helpful tips to share with her friends.

She's divided the book into several sections and even let her brothers and sister have their own chapters! You can find advice on roughing-it in Henry's Outdoor Adventures, crafts and art projects in Violet's Workbag, and, of course, delicious recipes in Benny's Belly. There are lots of things to explore, so let's get started!

Boxcar Tool Kit

There are always mysteries to solve and fun things to do! By using items found around the house or yard to build what we need, we are always prepared. Here are a few things to include in your Boxcar Tool Kit so you'll be ready for your next adventure!

Jessie Alden

REUSABLE WATER BOTTLE

Whether you're out and about on a hot day or need a quick wash-up, it never hurts to have water on hand. Some bottles come with clips that can attach to a backpack for easy carrying.

SEWING KIT
WITH A THREAD, NEEDLE, BUTTON, AND SAFETY PINS

Great when you need to mend a rip or turn some old clothes into a disguise. Be sure to have at least three safety pins—you'll want them for quick fixes.

BINDER CLIPS

These metal clips come in all sizes and are excellent for fastening things that won't hold together with a safety pin. Use them to keep curtains closed, seal up an unfinished bag of chips, or bookmark a book!

STRING

A foot or two of string can help when projects need a little more time to dry, or for a quick string game with a friend.

NOTEBOOK AND A PENCIL OR PEN

You never know when a great idea for a story will come. Use the notebook and pencil to sketch what you see on your adventure or to write down clues to remember.

TOTE BAG

Light fabric grocery bags can be rolled up as small as a fist. Keep one in your backpack to carry unexpected things like extra library books or garage sale treasures.

A SNACK
(SUCH AS A GRANOLA BAR)

Even adventurers get rumbly tummies like Benny.

SHOE MONEY

Keep a dollar or two folded in the bottom of your shoe. Who knows when you'll pass a lemonade stand or need fifty cents to fill your bike tires?

A GREAT BOOK!

Even adventurers get rumbly tummies like Benny!

CHAPTER ONE
Super Sleuths

Who's leaving notes in code at Lily's house? Did Bryan find animal tracks...or were those zombie footprints left in the mud? Mysteries are found in everyday adventures if you know where to look.

To help solve a mystery, form a *hypothesis* (an idea) to start you off on your investigation, and gather your clues. Look at all of the *evidence* (what proves something to be true), talk about what you've found with your family and friends, and make a solid guess as to what you think happened.

For example, I saw a large magpie, a type of bird, perched on top of the boxcar. The next day, Violet's favorite ring was missing from where she left it outside. After seeing a piece of metal glinting in the sunlight beneath a tree, she and I took a closer look. We knew that the birds love to steal shiny things, so our hypothesis was that the magpie took the ring. Our hypothesis was right—the ring was in the nest. Crafty birds!

What about that loud noise that you heard coming from the sky last night? Was it a plane? A distant clap of thunder? Or maybe a spaceship? It's time to break out your detective skills by asking the neighbors if they also heard the noise and if they saw anything such as lightning—or aliens. And don't forget to take pictures of what you find!

My siblings and I have discovered that things may not always be what they seem, but by using common sense, using what we have, and a little luck, we always get to the bottom of the mystery. Come to think of it, I think I know who took the last slice of apple pie. Benny!

Jessie Alden

Detective Kit

When you stumble upon a mystery, you'll need to think fast. Be ready with your own detective kit and jump into action!

FOR THE KIT, YOU'LL NEED:

- ☐ Backpack
- ☐ Notebook and pencil to record conversations (Be sure to note the time, the weather—rainy, sunny, snowy—the address or place where you are interviewing, and clues you come across.)
- ☐ Tape recorder for interviews
- ☐ Binoculars
- ☐ Camera
- ☐ Small bag of flour and a makeup brush to reveal fingerprints
- ☐ Tape to lift the fingerprint
- ☐ Blank index cards
- ☐ Soft tape measure to measure foot prints
- ☐ Tweezers to pick up evidence
- ☐ Small sealable bags to hold evidence
- ☐ Magnifying glass
- ☐ Snacks and water

How to investigate a mystery

Many investigations start by discussing what people saw, heard, or noticed missing. The *subject* is the person you will be asking questions to and writing down his or her answers.

❶ **Interviewing the subject:** Write down all that they can remember. While taking notes in your **notebook** from your detective kit, have the **voice recorder** running in the background as they speak. Play the recording back later to catch anything you may have missed. If you're trying to find out more about a certain event, ask the subject about where they were, who they were with, and what time it happened.

❷ **Who stole the cookie from the cookie jar?** If you're trying to find a missing object, have the owner describe it, and ask where they think it may have gone. Sometimes your best clues come from the owner herself.

❸   Sometimes you may find out who took a
     missing object by finding a fingerprint on a
     window or a dusty tabletop.
     To take a fingerprint: Using a *makeup brush*,
     press the bristles into a tiny bit of flour. Tap
     some *flour* onto where you suspect a fingerprint
     might be, such as on a glass, doorknob, or
     jewelry box, and gently brush it away with the
     makeup brush. The flour may reveal a fingerprint
     that doesn't match anyone in the house! Press
     the *tape* onto the fingerprint and lift it off the
     surface very carefully. This can be tricky so use a
     steady hand to lift the print! Stick the tape onto
     an *index card*, and write down where you took
     the print and the date. Keep the evidence in one
     of your *sealable bags* to keep it safe.

❹   Was it a zombie or your neighbor's dog
     looking for a treat?
     Check for footprints outside: You may be
     able to see footprints in soft soil or snow. Look
     around the outside of the house to see if there
     are any strange shoe prints. If there are, use a soft
     tape measure to see how large the shoe is and
     check to see if they match the shoes of anyone
     involved in the mystery.

⑤ **Sometimes a stray hair can unlock the mystery!**
Tiny clues: Use *tweezers* to pick up small
clues such as hair, fingernail clippings, or broken
jewelry, and place the objects into small sealable
bags for safekeeping. Don't forget to *label* the
bags with the date and where you found the clues.

⑥ **It's all in how you look at it.**
Go back and visit the site of the mystery during
different times of the day. You may see something
that was hidden in the shadows earlier or find
someone new to talk to about the riddle.

BOXCAR TIP

Make sure you have your parents' permission
before using their camera or binoculars on your
adventure!

BOXCAR TIP

Safety first! Never go
into a strange place
alone or follow
people you don't
know. Always tell
an adult before
you go on an
adventure so they
know where you are in
case you need backup.

Going Incognito: Disguises

Every good detective has a bag of disguises to change into just in case they've been discovered and need a quick getaway. Keep these items handy and you'll fool even the most determined ne'er-do-wells.

- ☐ Sunglasses
- ☐ Different colored shirt from the one you're wearing or a light jacket
- ☐ Hat
- ☐ Sneakers
- ☐ Eye patch
- ☐ Mustache

HOW TO MAKE
YOUR OWN MUSTACHE

I *mustache* you a question: what is
the quickest way for a detective to blend into the crowd
without being noticed? By changing their appearance
with a snappy mustache! Try curling the ends of a
brown, red, or black pipe cleaner, and securing to your
upper lip with a piece of tape. Or draw a bushy mustache
onto clear tape and stick it under your nose. Cut a
mustache shape out of sticky felt, then peel the paper
backing off the felt and apply above your lip for another
sly look. For a fluffier mustache, cut the shape out of
fake fur, then sew elastic or a ribbon to both ends and
wear securely around your head.

Mustaches may be dashing with wiggly ends or they can
be bushy and mysterious. It's better to have a few different
styles to choose from in your kit. In a pinch, extra
mustaches may be used as eyebrows, but choose wisely;
the curly ones are a dead giveaway and someone may
think you have a caterpillar growing out of your face.

classic   caterpillar   respectable

bushy   wiggly   funny

thin   extravagant   downward

Crack the Code

Mysterious notes are **appearing** and we're ready to solve the mystery. Can you help?

Writing codes, called **cryptography**, has been used for a very long time to send secret messages. Some messages are used to pass **secrets** from one person to another, while other codes are games. Codes may be made up of any symbols such as letters, numbers, or even squiggles. Putting them together forms a code and in order to read it, the other person needs a key to figure it out! **A key** consists of a graph that shows what each symbol represents.

REVERSE ALPHABET CODE

The alphabet code is written with letters in alphabetic order on one line, and the alphabet backward on the next line, so each letter's opposite is directly below it.

A B C D E F G H I J K L M N O P Q R S T U V W X Y Z

Z Y X W V U T S R Q P O N M L K J I H G F E D C B A

PIGPEN CODE

Draw two grids: one like a tic-tac-toe board and the other like a big X. Each letter is represented by the lines of the "pen" that it is in.

AB	CD	EF
GH	IJ	KL
MN	OP	QR

ST
UV   WX
YZ

When you want to use the second letter in the box like a B, D, or L, place a small dot next to the lines.

•⌐ = B

∨• = T

THE CLUE IN THE DARKROOM

In *The Mystery of the Secret Message (#55)*, Violet finds a photograph with a strange blank spot on it. The blank spot has been treated with a special chemical, so when the Aldens take it into a photography darkroom and dip the photo in water and expose it to light—suddenly, words appear!

GRID

Another great code is to use *a grid*. It may take a little time to write out, but once you get the hang of it, cracking codes is a snap.

Make a grid of five spaces down and five spaces across. Write the letters A, B, C, D, and E on the top of the grid and number the left column boxes 1 through 5. Starting with the letter F, write the letters in the remaining spaces left to right. To send a message to your friend, send them a code that matches the box like: 1B, 1E, 3D, 3D, 5E. To decipher the code, they simply need to match the boxes to your coded message.

1	A	B	C	D	E
2	F	G	H	I	J
3	K	L	M	N	O
4	P	Q	R	S	T
5	U	V	W	X	YZ

MIRROR WRITING

This is a bit trickier than the rest, but **writing in reverse** is a great way to confuse those with prying eyes. The artist Leonardo da Vinci used mirror writing to write some of his private notes. To see the message, others had to use a reflective surface like a mirror to read them.

To make your own mirror message, write your note on a piece of paper as usual. Then stand a hand mirror on its edge next to the paper so it reflects the backward writing. On another piece of paper, write down what you see in the mirror. Your friend will need to use a mirror to see what you've written! Some letters, like O or T look the same but others look crazy!

We found this note **hidden** in a **secret** room. What does it say? Use one of the keys to help us figure it out!

4E-2C-1E   1B-3E-5D   5C-2D-4E-2C

4E-2C-1E   2E-1E-5C-1E-3B   2D-4D

1B-5A-4C-2D-1E-1D   5A-3D-1D-1E-4C

4E-2C-1E   4A-3B-5A-3C   4E-4C-1E-1E

It looks like we have ***a mystery*** on our hands!

WHAT WAS THAT FLASHING LIGHT SAYING?

Morse code is a way to communicate using a series of dots and dashes to represent letters of the alphabet. We think it's a fun way for us to communicate at night without making a sound. By using our *flashlights*, I can tell Benny it's time for a late night snack or that someone is coming! A short burst of light is a dot, and a long flash is a dash. Pause for the count of three between letters, and pause for a count of five before making a new word so you don't get mixed up.

Make a copy of the code below for your friends and family so they can respond.

When it's daylight, try to whistle the code instead of using a flashlight or tap out the code with your fingers when your friend is nearby. What does this secret message say?

-- * * *　　-- -- --　　-- * * --　　-- * -- *　　*--　　* -- *

-- * -- *　　* * * *　　* *　　* -- * *　　-- * *

* -- *　　*　　-- *

A	* --	**J**	* -- -- --	**S**	* * *
B	-- * * *	**K**	-- * --	**T**	--
C	-- * -- *	**L**	* -- * *	**U**	* * --
D	-- * *	**M**	-- --	**V**	* * * --
E	*	**N**	-- *	**W**	* -- --
F	* * -- *	**O**	-- -- --	**X**	-- * * --
G	-- -- *	**P**	* -- -- *	**Y**	-- * -- --
H	* * * *	**Q**	-- -- * --	**Z**	-- -- * *
I	* *	**R**	* -- *		

How to Make Invisible Ink

Some things are for your best friend's eyes only! To make **invisible ink**, you will need:

- ❏ Tools to write with such as a cotton swab, paintbrush, or toothpick
- ❏ White paper
- ❏ Heat source such as a lightbulb or a sunny window
- ❏ Baking soda and water for Method 1
- ❏ The juice of a lemon for Method 2

METHOD 1:

❶ Mix equal parts **baking soda** and **water** together in a bowl.

❷ Using the baking soda mixture as your "ink," write your message onto the **paper** with your chosen detective **writing tool**.

> **OTHER PLACES THE ALDENS HAVE DISCOVERED MYSTERIOUS MESSAGES:**
>
> - Taped to the bottom of a table in a diner (#11)
> - On a candy heart (Special #18)
> - Inside a fortune cookie (#96)
> - On the side of a Ferris Wheel (#131)
> - On a marquee sign (#104)

❸ Wait for the paper to dry.

❹ Deliver to your best friend.

❺ Tell him that to see the secret message, he'll need to hold the paper over a **warm lightbulb**, but not to let the paper touch the bulb. The message will appear when the paper is warm.

METHOD 2:

❶ With help from an adult, cut a **lemon** in half and squeeze the juice into a bowl

❷ Using the lemon juice as your "ink," use your chosen **writing tool** to make a cool design or short message on the paper.

❸ Wait for the **paper** to dry.

❹ Deliver to your partner.

❺ Ask her to tape the paper onto a **sunny window** until the message appears in brown.

Now all you have to do is wait for them to write you back with their own messages!

Escape and Decoder Scarves

Violet and I love dressing up, and **scarves** are the perfect detective accessories. Women working as spies during World War II got double duty out of the fashionable fabric. The scarves of course protected their hair from the wind and rain. But printed on the reverse side of the fabric was an **escape route** of nearby towns, roads, and hideouts in case they needed to make a quick exit.

Sometimes, they would write down a **decoder key** onto the scarf. By tying it around their hair or neck, these spies held the answer to the mystery and no one was the wiser!

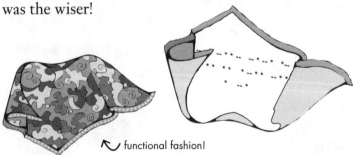

↶ functional fashion!

Whistles and Hand Signals

Was that a sparrow outside your window or a **secret message** between two master detectives? When you're out in the field and need to quickly communicate with your team fast, **a whistle** can alert them to be ready to roll.

WHISTLE SIGNALS

One long, low whistle means to be quiet and listen for the next signal.

A few long, slow whistles means to get farther away or to scatter and not be found.

A few short, quick blasts mean to come back together as a group or to join you.

A long whistle followed by **a short one**, then **another long** and **another short** means to look out!

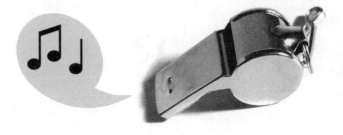

HAND SIGNALS

If you can see your partner but are unable to make a sound, *hand signals work* just as well.

Swinging your arm from your back to front means to move in or get closer to the person or persons you are following.

Circling your arm around your head tells your team to retreat and head back to base.

To stop the team, *raise your arm* above your head and point up to the sky.

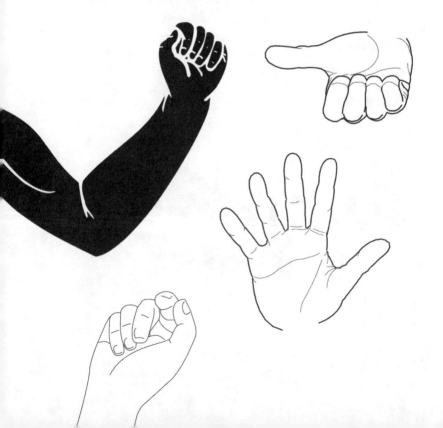

Secret Handshakes

The handshake started as a gesture of peace, to show that neither person was going to poke the other with a stick if he got too close. It is now used as a way to say **hello**, to **congratulate** someone on a job well done, and to **seal a deal**. Handshakes are also used to show that a person is part of a **secret club**. Each wiggle of a finger may be part of a code!

Make up a secret handshake with your friends and family. Get creative by using your whole body with elbow bumps, fish faces, and snazzy dance moves as you learn the code together. Will **a wink** mean it's time for lunch? Or can **a thumb dance** tell you to meet your friend after school by the elm tree? Keep it simple at first, and then move to fancier footwork as you learn more steps.

We don't recommend you try this one at home.

CHAPTER TWO
Outdoor Adventures

SEVEN BOXCAR CHILDREN MYSTERIES ABOUT THE GREAT OUTDOORS!

#3, *Yellow House Mystery*
#9, *Mountain-Top Mystery*
#27, *The Camp-Out Mystery*
#40, *The Canoe Trip Mystery*
#61, *The Growling Bear Mystery*
#76, *The Great Bicycle Race Mystery*
#86, *The Mystery on Blizzard Mountain*

BOXCAR TIP

Be safe! Always have an adult with you when walking away from the group and while setting up camp.

Before we met our grandfather, we started our adventures by taking shelter in a **boxcar**. We loved being in the wilderness, because there were so many things to do. Now that Grandfather has moved the boxcar to our backyard, we're still able to visit and play in our snug little hideaway. Here are some of the things we learned while exploring outdoors.

Jessie Alden

Tents

When not in the boxcar, we love sleeping in a **roomy tent**. We like to put the tent up as a team since it can be difficult to manage poles by ourselves. So grab a brother and a sister or a few friends and get started!

UNPACKING THE TENT

Before setting up the tent, make sure you have all of the equipment needed. Most tents will have the following:

- ☐ Inner tent
- ☐ Tent poles
- ☐ Outer tent
- ☐ Pegs

YOU MAY ALSO NEED

- ☐ Hammer—or use a rock or other heavy item if you don't have a hammer
- ☐ Tarp

PICKING A GREAT CAMPSITE

Look for a **flat and dry** area. Keep away from anywhere
that may flood if it starts raining. You don't want to wake
up in a puddle! **Clear the space** of all fallen branches,
twigs, and rocks since those can be very uncomfortable
to sleep on.

Where's the best place to look? **Mountaintops** can be
quite windy while valleys may gather dew in the early
morning and you may wake up damp and groggy. Try
to find a campsite that is in between. If you're in the
backyard, find a nice **sunny spot**.

SETTING UP THE TENT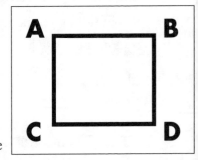

If you brought a **tarp**, lay that down first. This helps to
protect your tent from tree roots poking up from the
ground or any moisture from dew. Place the corners

of your inner tent on top of
the tarp and spread them out
evenly. If the tarp is too big,
tuck it under the sides of the
tent. Put **pegs** in the loops
found on the corners of your
tent and hammer them into the
ground securely starting with

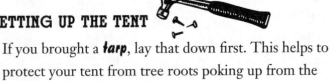

opposite corners such as A then D, then C and B:

If there are more than four pegs, **hammer** those into the
ground next.

POLES

With help from a friend, put the **poles** together. Some may be long and heavy, while others click together easily, depending on the tent. Run the poles through the guides on the outside of the tent and watch it begin to take shape!

OUTER TENT

The **outer tent** is used in case of rainfall and as an added layer of privacy. On sunny days, you may choose to leave the outer tent off and unzip the tent window flaps for a nice breeze through the screens. To use the outer tent, ask an adult to toss it over the top so you can secure the strings or poles to the ground, or clip it to the inner tent poles.

PUTTING THE TENT AWAY

After your campout, it's important to put the tent back properly.

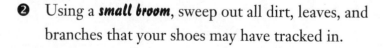

❶ First, remove everything from the tent.

❷ Using a **small broom**, sweep out all dirt, leaves, and branches that your shoes may have tracked in.

❸ Pull the **pegs** out of the ground and clean them off before storing them. It helps to have the pegs in their own **zippered bag** to find them easily next time.

❹ Remove the **poles** and break them down.

❺ Lay the **tent** out flat and fold one side to the other like you're folding a giant towel into sections. Repeat folding until it is small enough to place into its bag.

❻ Don't forget to include the pegs and poles into the **carrier bag** with the tent!

❼ Fold the **tarp**.

❽ Before you leave your campsite, take another look around to make sure you left the area cleaner than how you found it. No litter!

Always have the zippers to the entrance closed on your tent! You don't want little buzzers to invade your space and make it hard to sleep!

TENT KEEPING

After the tent is up, it's time to move in! Benny loves to bring his stuffed bear while Violet likes to bring along a book and her camera for those perfect nature photos. I make sure we bring everything we need to have a safe and cozy time in the tent.

❑   Sleeping bags. If it's going to be extra cold during the night, bring an ***extra blanket*** to put inside the sleeping bag for added warmth. No sleeping bag? Make a ***jelly roll***! Roll up your blanket and sheet together into a big roll and tuck it into your pillowcase along with your pillow for a quick snooze on the road.

❑   Sleeping pad or air mattress. Boy, that ground can be hard! If you (or your parents) don't want creaky bones in the morning, bring along a ***thick foam pad*** or an ***inflatable air mattress*** to sleep on.

❑   Flashlight for flashlight tag, shadow puppets, or a night hike

❑   Food and plenty of water

❑   Dishes

❑   Trash bag for your recyclables and one for trash, to keep them separate and ready to dispose of when you leave

❑   Bug spray or bug towelettes

❑   Books and board games

Campfire songs

Henry and Benny love to sing songs while we're out helping a neighbor or traveling with Grandfather. Here are a few of our favorites. Which one do you like best?

HEADS, SHOULDERS, KNEES, AND TOES

This is a *fun* one! When you name each part of the body, touch them with your fingers. The second time you sing the verse, leave out the word "head" but still do the hand movement, while the third time you sing the song, leave out the word "shoulders." Repeat the song until you have no more body parts to name and it's all actions with no words. Speed up the song to make it even more challenging (and giggle-inducing).

Head, shoulders, knees, and toes, knees and toes,
Head, shoulders, knees, and toes, knees and toes,
Eyes and ears and mouth and nose,
Head, shoulders, knees, and toes, knees and toes!

BOOM CHICKA-BOOM

This song has one song leader and the rest of the group sings it back to her before starting the next verse.

I said boom chicka-boom!
(repeat back to song leader)

I said boom chicka-boom!
(repeat back to song leader)

I said boom-chicka-rocka-chicka-rocka-chicka-boom!
(repeat back to song leader)

Uh huh! Oh yeah! One more time!
(name a type of boom chicka-boom below)

❑ Underwater style (sing with fingers dribbling against your lips)

❑ Baby style (in a baby voice and with your thumb in your mouth)

❑ Opera style (high wobbly voice)

❑ Janitor style (I said broom sweepa-broom! I said broom sweepa-broom! I said broom-sweepa-mopa-sweepa-mopa-sweepa-broom!)

❑ Photographer style (I said zoom chica-zoom, I said zoom chica-zoom! I said zoom chica-chicka-chicka-chica-zoom! Of course, this is Violet's favorite verse!)

❑ Make up your own style!

THE BEAR SONG

This silly song starts with the song leader saying one verse, and then you repeat it back to him or her. When the verse is complete, sing it all together before singing the next verse.

The other day
I met a bear
Out in the woods
Oh way out there

He looked at me
I looked at him
He sized up me
I sized up him

He said to me
Why don't you run
I see you ain't
Got any gun

I said to him
That's a good idea
So come on, feet,
Away from here

And so I ran
Away from there
But right behind
Me was that bear

And then I see
Ahead of me
A great big tree
Oh, glory be!

The lowest branch
Was ten feet up
I'd have to jump
And trust my luck!

And so I jumped
Into the air
But I missed that branch
A way up there

Now don't you fret
Now don't you frown
'Cause I caught that branch
On the way back down

This is the end
There ain't no more
Until I meet
That bear once more

How to catch a fish

Catching a fish for your supper or to release back into the water is so much fun! Henry is a great fisherman and I'm learning too! We can learn together starting with these simple tools:

- ❑ Fishing pole
- ❑ Fishhook
- ❑ Bobber
- ❑ Weights (if needed)

- ❑ Bait
- ❑ Basket
- ❑ Net

LOCATION

Streams, lakes, and ponds are great places to check out. Look for a nice shady spot to get started. You can also check the local newspaper for fishing reports. Many times, they will tell you which spots are best, what kind of fish are biting, and what the fish love to nibble on!

BOXCAR TIP

Be sure to check if you need a fishing license before heading to the water. A fishing license can be purchased by an adult at many local stores or online.

HOOKS

Buy hooks that will fit snugly into a fish's mouth. The best fishers have tackle boxes full of different hooks for catching specific fish. But a simple #1 hook should work well for many types of fish. Be careful, hooks can be very sharp! Ask an adult for help tying the fishing line onto the hook with a good strong knot.

BAIT

Worms, grasshoppers, fish roe (fish eggs), and bacon can make a fish extra hungry. If bait jiggles or smells, the fish are interested. To find your own bait, take a bucket filled with soil and check the lawn and sidewalks after a good rainstorm. Worms will wiggle their way up to the surface and you can plop them into your bait bucket. If you're leaving for a fishing trip early the next morning, take a flashlight and shine it onto the grass in your backyard the night before since worms may be on top of the soil enjoying the cool evening air.

GETTING YOUR POLE READY

Attach the hook to the fishing line. If you're fishing in a swift stream, attach a weight or *sinker* about one foot above your hook and bait. This allows your hook to sink but still keeps it away from the rocks so the hook is less likely to get caught.

If you're fishing near a slow river or lake, use a bobber or cork above your baited hook. The bobber tells you where the hook is and keeps your bait from sinking to the bottom of the lake.

TIME TO FISH!

Drop your line into the water by *casting*, meaning you very carefully throw the hook into the water by holding onto the pole and pitching the line like you would a softball. Keep a hold of that pole so it doesn't go into the water! If you're in a boat, just drop the hook over the edge. Now it's time to wait.

And wait.

And wait.

Patience is a big part of fishing, just like detective work. Keep a sharp eye out for any movement of the bobber or line, and when you feel a tug, it's time to reel it in! To *set* the hook, give your pole a swift tug upward. If you feel a weight on the other end, you may have caught a fish! Pull the fish to shore or into the boat by tugging and spinning the reel on the fishing pole. When the fish is close enough, use a net to scoop it up so it won't flop back into the water.

REMOVING THE HOOK

Ask an adult to remove the hook from your fish's mouth.
If you plan to eat your catch for supper, add water to a
bucket and put the fish inside to stay fresh. You can also
use a small wicker basket or *creel* instead of a bucket. Or
take a photograph of you with your fish and release it
back into the water and start again!

Hiking

Hiking is an excellent way to explore the wilderness!
Check out the trails with an adult and get ready for
adventure. Be in the know before you go with these
handy tips.

❶ Beginning hikers should start with a short
distance, usually a mile or so, and work up to
longer trips. That way, your feet are ready and
your legs won't get so wobbly down the road.

❷ Wear a good pair of shoes and socks. Be prepared
to climb over rocks and jump a stream or two
with shoes that have good support. Sore feet
come from flat-soled shoes like flip-flops, while
blisters appear in a jiffy without socks, so make
your trip memorable for what you see and not
how much your feet hurt.

❸ If going on a longer hike, take a small daypack
to carry your essentials: first-aid kit, compass,
sketch pad and pencil, water bottle or canteen,
bandana, a whistle, and a snack such as a granola
bar, an orange, nuts, string cheese, or trail mix.
Fruits like oranges and lemons are a great way to
keep hydrated during the hike!

PACK YOUR FIRST AID KIT WITH:

☐ Bandages

☐ Cotton swabs

☐ Triple antibiotic ointment

☐ Eye drops

☐ Tweezers in case of splinters

☐ Moleskin to cover blisters. Use as soon as you as you see
a blister develop to help stop it in its tracks. Duct tape may
also be used to cover a "hot spot" in a pinch.

☐ Bug spray

☐ Chewable allergy tablets

☐ Resealable baggies

HITTING THE TRAIL

Always have an adult with you before you set out, and
make sure everyone knows the rules: no running ahead
where an adult cannot see you, use the buddy system,

take a rest break together, and don't explore too far from your home base. Now let's get out there!

Part of our job as detectives is being able to read clues.

Native Americans and early settlers used simple signs to show where they traveled to mark the trail for others. When you're hiking, see if you can find clues that other walkers have left for you, and then leave a few of these trail

Keep going   Danger! Stop!

Go left   Go right

Go this way   Go the other way

signals along the path for your friends to follow!

Trail signs may be made of things found along the road such as rocks, branches, feathers, and flowers. When you make your trail sign, be sure it is visible along the path so no one misses it while they walk.

Directions

USING YOUR COMPASS

There are four directions on a compass: north, east, south, and west. They are called the cardinal points. Halfway between those markings are called intermediate directions. They are northeast, southeast, southwest, and northwest. Use your compass to help guide you while using a map or geocaching.

FINDING DIRECTIONS WITHOUT A COMPASS

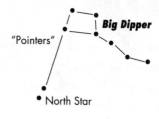

By the sun: The sun rises in the east and sets in the west. By noon, the sun is directly overhead and a tiny bit to the south in the Northern Hemisphere. So if you are facing the sun at that time, you're headed south and north is behind you.

By the stars: Our solar system has one star that remains constantly fixed while the rest seem to revolve as the Earth spins. It's called the North Star or the Pole Star. To find the North Star, find the two stars (also called *pointer stars*) on the outer edge of the cup end of the Big Dipper and follow them straight to the North Star. It's not very bright, so it takes practice to find. But once you do, it'll be a snap to find it again!

Always stay with your group. But if you find yourself lost, don't panic and stay put! Hug a tree and wait for your group to find you. Use your whistle from your pack to help them get to you quickly.

Watch loves to come with us on the trail! If you're bringing your pet on a hike, make sure to check with the park officials first for permission. And be sure to bring extra supplies for your four-legged friend!

Going on a night hike

Hiking with your family and friends under a full moon is a fun way to see the trail in a whole new light—moonlight, that is! It's a great way to see the stars, plus hear and see animals that are out and about at night such as owls, fireflies, opossums, and bats.

With your eyesight limited to what you can see in the glow of the headlamp or flashlight, you'll learn to trust your other senses. Can you hear the frogs and crickets? Or use your fingers to touch a moonflower as it opens its petals? Moonflowers only open at night so act fast—as soon as the sun rises, the moonflower will close its bloom up tight until the next cool evening!

Before you leave on your nighttime adventure, make a list of things to do with your family when not stargazing:

❑   Scavenger hunt. Break into teams to photograph nocturnal animals like owls, raccoons, or bats; a particular type of tree; or animal tracks.

❑   I Spy. This game is trickier at night, so keep your eyes peeled!

❑   Songs

❑   Silly stories

PREPARING FOR A NIGHT HIKE

Getting ready for your night hike is
similar to getting ready for a day hike. Plan
your hike before you leave so everyone
stays on the trail and knows how to get
back to your house or campsite. It's very
important to stay with an adult during a
night hike, but if you do become separated,
remember to hug a tree and use the whistle in your
backpack to help others find you. Along with the whistle,
be sure to bring a jacket, first-aid kit, bug spray, camera
or sketchbook and pencil, headlamp to keep your hands
free, a water bottle or canteen, and snacks. Pack a set of
extra batteries for the headlamp just in case it goes dim
while you're on your hike.

Pick a trail that you've been on during the day.
It's fun to see how different it becomes when the
sun goes down. Stay away from trails that cross
streams or that are too rocky. The best trails at
night are the ones that have a big open view of
the sky so you can count the stars.

Start your hike before the sun is fully set.
You'll have a chance to photograph or sketch
the sunset in your notebook before it gets too
dark, and your eyes will become adjusted to the
dimming light quicker.

When you're out on the trail, listen for sounds that you don't normally hear when the sun is shining.

Owls have a long, low sound like a "whooooo" or a screeching noise. Barred owls make a "whoo whoo whoo whooooooo" sound. Other noises you might hear can sound like a baby crying or a raspy bark that doesn't sound like a dog's. These belong to a fox. You might also hear the chirp of a katydid or the northern mockingbird enjoying the moonlight while the rest of the animal kingdom sleeps.

BOXCAR TIP

Animals that hunt during the night are called *nocturnal animals,* and they usually sleep during the daytime. At night, it's time for them to hunt their prey so be careful where you step!

MONSTER TRACKS?

In *Mystery in the Cave (#50),* Benny sees a strange set of tracks—giant footprints and then a long mark like something dragged on the ground. Benny thinks it's a monster, dragging its tail! (Jessie isn't so sure.)

A night hike can be exciting—and tiring.
Start with a short hike and work your way up to longer ones then be sure to get a good night's sleep. Look at that! Benny's already snoozing!

Animal tracks

Animal tracks are imprints left by creatures in snow, mud, or soft soil. By learning what kinds of animals left their prints behind, we can tell what walked the path before us. It takes a sharp eye to see some of the smaller prints! The best place to find prints will be near the water when animals go for a drink or a swim. The soil is soft and mushy, perfect for tiny toes to make a deep impression.

BOXCAR TIP

To share your find, take a photograph or sketch it in your notebook to show your friends!

BOXCAR TIP

Be careful of following prints into a den. The animal could be inside and may not be in the mood for company!

15 Uses for a Bandana

Who knew that this little scrap of colored fabric can be so handy? I've listed fifteen here but there are dozens of ways to put it to use. What's your favorite?

❶ Dishcloth

❷ Sassy headband

❸ Lunch box

❹ Tie the corners of two bandanas together to make a quick pillow case for a square pillow

❺ Place mat for your picnic lunch

❻ Tie the opposite corners together to make a small bag to carry shells, souvenirs, or a book

❼ Mask

❽ Eye patch

❾ Belt

❿ Washcloth

⓫ Handkerchief

⓬ Emergency baby diaper

⓭ Hat

⓮ Fill with ice to use as a cold compress

⓯ Hand puppet

ANOTHER USE FOR A BANDANA...
In *Mystery in the Cave (#50)* Violet makes a safety flag while the Aldens are cave exploring by tying a bandana around a stick to mark a hole in the ground!

Forts

There was nothing as snug as our little boxcar during those nights in the woods, but we love making forts too! Create your own space indoors with cushions and blankets to make a fun place to read a book, listen to music, or tell secrets with your friends.

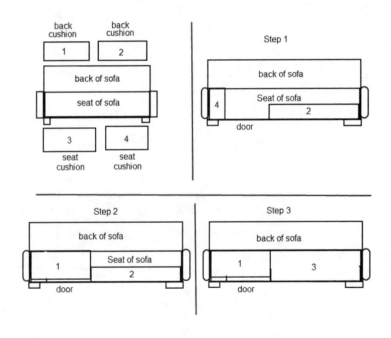

SOFA FORT

Constructing a fort from sofa cushions is a breeze with just a few cushions and using the sofa as a base.

❶ Remove cushions from the couch.

❷ You will have two back cushions (numbers 1 & 2) and two seat cushions (numbers 3 & 4).

❸ Wedge seat cushion number 4 next to the left arm of the sofa so that it stands up and creates a wall.

❹ Take back cushion number 2 and place it on the edge of the base of the sofa. You may need a friend to hold it steady or use a chair to keep it from tipping over.

❺ Use back cushion number 1 as a roof by balancing it on top of cushions 2 and the end of cushion 4, using the back of the sofa as another wall.

❻ Finally, place seat cushion number 3 to complete the fort by balancing the cushion on top of the back of the sofa and cushion number 4.

❼ For added privacy, cover the fort with a blanket or tablecloth.

❽ Enter your fort through the front door and snuggle up with a Boxcar Children book!

TABLE FORT

The dining room table isn't just for supper! Throw a
large sheet or a few long tablecloths over your dining
room table for a roomy fort that's just the right place to
spend a rainy afternoon.

BUNK BED FORT

This reminds me of the boxcar! Tuck a blanket or extra
sheet between the mattress and the base of the upper
bunk and let the ends fall down to the ground. It gets
dark in there so pack a flashlight for a late-night read.

EASY TREE HOUSE FORT

This fort is a snap! Tie the end of a line of rope to the
lowest branch of a large tree and secure the other end to
another branch. Using clothespins, pin sheets along the
rope to create walls. Make extra rooms by adding more
rope and sheets or run the line to another nearby tree
and make a maze!

BOXCAR CARDBOARD FORT

What to do with that giant box? Race car? Suit of armor?
How about a boxcar? Next time you get your hands
on a big cardboard box, ask an adult to cut out a door
and windows to make a quick and easy fort. Decorate

the box with red paint, markers, and stickers to make it your own. Add some large throw pillows inside and your favorite blanket for a cozy getaway just like ours. Have two boxes? Have a friend or sibling decorate their own box and you can become neighbors.

FORT-TO-FORT COMMUNICATION

If you have two forts and want to communicate between them, or if you want to talk to a person outside the fort before she's allowed in, you can make your own telephone! Take two large paper cups and make a tiny hole in the center of the base with a needle. Thread thin string (like kite string) between the two cups. Knot the ends of the string inside of each cup and pull it tight against the bottom. For extra strength, tape the knot to the bottom of the cup. Stretch the string between you and your friend. Make sure the string is tight—but don't pull too hard, the string may pop through the cup—and listen as your friend talks into the cup. What do you hear?

CHAPTER THREE
On the Go!

THOSE TRAVELING ALDENS

Here are just some of the places the Boxcar Children have visited. Have you been to any of these places too?

San Antonio
San Francisco
New York City
Chicago
Yellowstone National Park
Florida Everglades

London
Washington, DC
Seattle
Outer Banks
   of North Carolina
Niagara Falls

We love to travel with Grandfather when he visits friends or when we are on school vacations. Try these travel games with your family and watch the miles go by with smiles.

Map: Trips are always more fun if you have a plan. Before you leave, find out more about your route with the help of an adult and create your own map! Draw the road you'll be taking on paper, and don't forget fun places to visit on the way such as parks, monuments, and your favorite restaurants. When you visit each place, draw a picture of it in your notebook so you can share it with your friends when you get home.

Secret messages: With a friend, ask him or her to draw a letter or number on your palm while you have your eyes closed. Was it a K? How about a C? After you've guessed the right letter or number, it's your friend's turn. For more of a challenge, draw short two- or three-letter words onto her palm and see if she can guess it correctly.

Foil fun: Aluminum foil can be molded into lots of shapes. Bring a box along to make your own super hero mask and shield, a crown, jewelry, or twist the foil into animal figures like monkeys, snails, or our dog, Watch!

Make your own story: What will your trip be like? Who will you see? Will there be zombies? The adventure is just starting, so write down what you think your trip will be like and who you'll meet each day. Then at the end of the trip, compare the story with what really happened.

ABC animals: Keep an eye out for animals on your trip in this fast-moving game. Start with the letter A and the first to see an animal whose name starts with that letter yells out the name of that animal (such as an ant). Then move on to B until you've finished the alphabet. Some letters are tricky, like X and Q, so have a good back-up plan ready (like you saw a queen bee).

License plate game: Look for different states, letters, or even colors in the license plates on other cars while on a road trip. You can give extra points for the car from the farthest state away.

Secret word game: Before the trip begins, choose a special word, like "hippopotamus," for example. When the word is spoken, each member puts a finger on his or her nose. The last person to touch his nose is in charge of slipping the word into the conversation.

Guess who: Think of a person everyone on the trip knows. Describe that person in five words or less. Does she have brown hair? Six fingers on one hand? Does she snort when she laughs or make the best homemade peach ice cream ever? Whoever guesses that person first is the next to have a turn.

I Spy: "I spy with my little eye something…green." Since moving cars and small objects can be hard to spot as you drive by, the best way to play this game in the car is to choose something large, like a sign or landmark that your car mates can see for at least a few minutes. If you play I Spy while out walking, you have more chances to be tricky, like choosing a flower or a button on your brother's shirt. To shake it up a little, start with saying, "I spy with my little eye, something that starts with (a letter) or is big like (a big example)." The first person to name the object is the next player.

Car Tunes: Each person takes a turn humming a song or a theme song from their favorite television show. The person that guesses correctly is the next to go!

How to Pack a Suitcase

My siblings and I are always ready for an adventure, but first we have to pack! I like to keep organized and tidy with these tricks to filling a suitcase.

❶ First choose a suitcase big enough for your trip. A backpack for an overnight slumber party works well but if you'll be gone longer, you may want a larger suitcase.

❷ Make a list:

- ❏ Pants
- ❏ Shirts
- ❏ Swimsuit
- ❏ Pajamas
- ❏ Underwear
- ❏ Socks
- ❏ Sweater or jacket
- ❏ Shoes

❸ Pack your suitcase by laying the case on a flat surface.

LAYER ONE

T-shirts and jeans are the bulkiest items to pack, so start with those first.

❶ Lay each of your shirts on top of one another in a pile. Roll them up together like a big hot dog beginning with the bottoms until you reach the collars. Place the roll on the bottom of your suitcase.

❷ Softer items like sweatpants or cotton pants may be folded lengthwise and rolled the same way as the shirts.

❸ Roll up jeans one by one and put them on the bottom layer next to your shirts and other pants.

LAYER TWO

Your next layer holds clothes that are easily wrinkled like fancy shirts and dresses. Fold those by laying the shirt facedown on the bed. Fold the arms of the shirt toward the middle until they touch, then fold the bottom of the shirt up until it reaches the shoulders of the shirt. Carefully flip it over and put it into your suitcase on top of the hot dogs—I mean, the rolled shirts and pants.

LAYER THREE

Roll up socks and underwear into balls and tuck into the corners of the case. Stick a few of the socks inside of your shoes and pack the shoes into the corners of the suitcase, along the sides, or in an outer pocket.

When you've finished packing, drop the suitcase or bag on the ground. **Gravity will help settle the clothes** and you'll have more room to pack in your favorite stuffed animal or an extra book!

Heavy shoes and coats can take up a lot of room in your suitcase so wear the bulky items instead of packing them.

Up in the Air with the Aldens

Flying across the country can be exciting—and tiring. Plan ahead with tips to make the trip fun and easy breezy.

Along with your suitcase, fill a small carry-on, such as a backpack, with items to make the time go faster.

INCLUDE ANY OF THE FOLLOWING:

❏ Notebook for drawing pictures, stories, tic-tac-toe, hangman, or other written games

❏ Pencil or pen

- ☐ Crayons or colored pencils
- ☐ Stickers
- ☐ A book or e-reader
- ☐ Handheld gaming device
- ☐ Music player with earbuds

candy will make it hard to stay in your seat!

- ☐ Snacks like string cheese, an apple, pretzels, dried fruit, or a granola bar
- ☐ Magazines
- ☐ Homework
- ☐ Favorite stuffed animal or small toys
- ☐ Small pillow for a quick rest
- ☐ A change of clothes, like a T-shirt and pants
- ☐ Gum or mints to chew while the plane takes off into the air and when it lands. The gum will help your ears pop and make the change in air pressure within the plane more comfortable. Extra points if it's bubble gum and you have the biggest bubble!

BOXCAR TIP

To find things easily, separate electronics, snacks, writing tools, and books into resealable zippered bags. It makes finding what you are looking for a cinch!

IS THAT YOUR BAG?

Lots of suitcases and bags look the same. In *The Mystery of the Queen's Jewels* (Special #11), someone on the Aldens' flight to London mistakes Benny's backpack for his own. Make sure you have the right bag or else you might cause an international mystery!

BEFORE YOU BOARD THE PLANE

Airports can be exciting places to explore but stay with your parents at all times. Often, there are kids' playgrounds found in the terminals. Make a game with your family to see who can find it first.

You'll be seated for a while as you glide through the clouds. Why not find out who can do the silliest walk while you wait in the terminal for your flight? It will help get the wiggles—and the giggles—out.

WHILE SEATED ON THE PLANE

Help others around you enjoy the flight by being respectful and helping your little siblings get settled. Read them their favorite Boxcar Children book or start a game of tic-tac-toe in your notebook.

During the flight, always ask your parent's permission before playing with the television screen on the back of the seats if your plane has them. Your parents or the flight attendants can show you how to use the monitors and how to find the channels you'd like to see. Be sure to take a break between shows with a quiet game of I Spy, a quick nap, or another chapter in your book.

Airplane travel can make you extra thirsty! Instead of soda or juice, ask the flight attendant for water to keep your body hydrated and happy.

ARRIVAL

Once the plane has landed, check around your seat and in the seat pocket in front of you to make sure you have everything tucked away in your backpack. Throw away any trash when the flight attendant brings a bag down the aisle to keep your row tidy. As you exit your row, make sure to look for any crayons, small toys, or books that may have fallen into the cracks between the seats.

Learning the Lingo

Traveling to a new place is exciting, but can be a little confusing if you're not familiar with the language. Before you head out on your trip, practice some of these words and phrases so you'll be in the know before you go. Even if you're not traveling, you can pretend to visit different countries by learning the language!

SPANISH

Hello: Hola (oh-lah)

Good morning: Buenos días (bway-nohs dee-ahs)

Good night: Buenas noches (bway-nahs noh-chays)

Good-bye: Adiós (ah-dee-ohs)

Please: Por favor (por fah-bor)

Thank you: Gracias (grah-see-ahs)

You're welcome: De nada (day nah-dah)

Excuse me: Perdón (pehr-dohn)

Yes: Sí (see)

No: No (noh)

Friend: Amigo (ah-mee-go)

Spain's flag colors: yellow and red

FRENCH

Hi: Salut (saw-loo)

Good morning:
Bonjour (bon zhoor)

Good evening:
Bonsoir (bon swar)

Good-bye:
Au revoir (oh reh-vwar)

Please: S'il vous plaît
(see voo play)

Thank you:
Merci (mair-see)

You're welcome:
De rien (du-rhee-en)

Excuse me: Excusez-moi
(escoosay mwah)

Yes: Oui (whee)

No: Non (no)

Friend: Ami (ah-mee)

France's flag colors: blue, white, and red

GERMAN

Hello:
Guten Tag (goo-ten tahk)

Good morning:
Guten Morgen
(goo-ten morgen)

Good night: Gute Nacht
(goo-ten nahdt)

Good-bye:
Auf Wiedersehen
(owf vee-der-zay-en)

Please: Bitte (bitt-uh)

Thank you:
Danke (danh-kuh)

You're welcome:
Bitte schön
(bitt-uh shurn)

Excuse me:
Entschuldigen Sie
(ehnt-shool-dih-gun zee)

Yes: Ja (yah)

No: Nein (nine)

Friend: Freund (froynt)

ITALIAN

Good day: Buon giorno
(bwohn jour-noh)

Good evening: Buona
sera (bwoh-nah sair-rah)

Good-bye: Arrivederci
(ah-ree-vah-dair-chee)

Please: Per favore
(pair fa-vohr-ray)

Thank you: Grazie
(grat-tzee-yay)

You're welcome:
Prego (pray-go)

Excuse me:
Scusi (skoo-zee)

Yes: Sì (see)

No: No (noh)

Friend:
Amico (ah-mee-co)

Italy's flag colors: green, white, and red

JAPANESE

Hello: Konnichiwa
(kohn-nee-chee-wah)

Good morning:
Ohayo (oh-hah-yoh)

Good evening:
Konbanwa
(kohn-bahn-wah)

Good-bye: Sayonara
(sye-yoh-nah-rah)

Please (when asking
for something): Onegai
shimasu (oh-neh-gye
shee-moss)

Thank you:
Domo arigato (doh-moh
ah-ree-gah-toh)

You're welcome:
Dou itashimashite
(doh ee-tah-shee mosh-the)

Excuse me: Sumimasen
(sue-mee-mah-sehn)

Yes: Hai (high)

No: Iie (EE-yeh)

Friend: Tomodachi
(toh-moh-dah-chee)

SWAHILI

Hello: Jambo (jam-bo)

Good morning: Habari ya asubuhi (huh-hab-ree ah-soo-boo-hee)

Good night: Usiku mwema (oo-see-koo mm-weh-mah)

Uganda's flag colors: black, yellow, and red

Good-bye: Kwaheri (kwah-hey-ree)

Please: Tafadhali (tah-fah-dah-lee)

Thank you: Asante (ah-san-tee)

You're welcome: Karibu (kah-ree-boo)

Excuse me: Samahani (sah-ma-ha-nee)

Yes: Ndiyo (nndee-yoh)

No: Hapana (ha-pa-na)

Friend: Rafiki (rah-fee-kee)

Tanzania's flag colors: green, yellow, black, and blue

SWEET TALK

Did you know that French is spoken in Quebec, a province of Canada? In *The Mystery of the Screech Owl*, the Boxcar Children visit a village in Quebec where maple syrup is made. There they try *tarte du sucre*—maple sugar pie!

68

AMERICAN SIGN LANGUAGE

Try spelling out your answers using American Sign Language. This is known as "finger spelling."

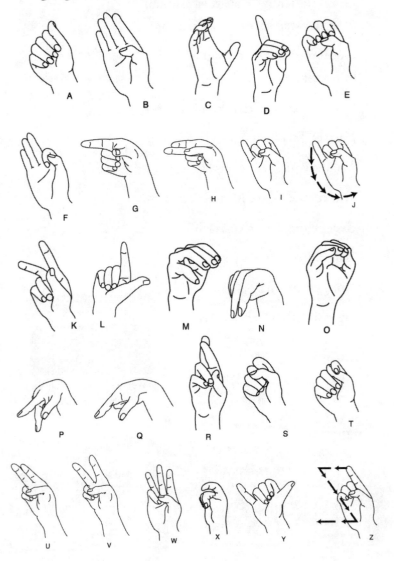

Say Cheese! How to take great digital photographs

Violet loves photography! Going on vacation means lots of opportunities to capture a fun moment with your family and friends. Get permission from an adult first to use their camera or camera phone and start snapping!

❶ Try different angles in your shots. Get up close to a bug or stand at the base of a tree and take a photo underneath the branches for a different perspective. Take a photo from the other side of your subject. What does the back of your mom's head look like? You'll learn to train your eyes to see more than just one point of view.

❷ Keep the background simple. Too many things behind your subject can be distracting. Try to have a clear background, like the sky or a wall, so the star of the photo is your subject—and not a plant growing out of his or her ear.

❸ Have an adult teach you the best way to hold the camera so your photo isn't shaky. Prop the camera up on a table or other firm object, or lean against something sturdy so you aren't wobbly, and shoot. It takes a little practice so don't be discouraged if you get a few of your fingers in the shot!

❹ Take different subjects in photographs. Try people in some and buildings or nature in others. Take photos of what is interesting to you. Those will be the best memories to share later.

❺ The best time to take outdoor photographs is in the early morning or late afternoon. The sun's light isn't as harsh and you won't have your brother squinting into the camera.

❻ Find a focal point in your photograph. A focal point is what you like the most in the picture you're about to take, like your dad or a kitten. Focus on how you'd like them to be in the photo: against a tree, catching an ocean wave on a boogie board (hard for a kitten), or even sitting next to you on the airplane wearing goofy headphones.

❼ For more fun, add a theme to your photo adventure. Ask your family to make the same silly pose at each monument you visit, or hold up a sign saying where you are so you can create a scrapbook when you get home.

A Treasure Hunt in a Box: Geocaching

Who's ready for a treasure hunt? *Geocaching*, or letterboxing, is a fun way to explore new places and use our mapping skills. Find clues online and see if you can find your own buried treasure, and then leave your own!

To find a geocache, go online with a parent to geocaching.com. There you will find clues and tips to find hidden caches all over the world. Using the clues and the GPS on your smartphone, you'll be able to find and trade goodies and log in your find. Always leave the cache in the same spot you found it so the next treasure hunter will have the same luck!

TO LEAVE A CACHE, YOU'LL NEED A FEW SUPPLIES:

- ❑ A waterproof container
- ❑ Plastic bag to protect the contents
- ❑ Logbook
- ❑ Pencil
- ❑ Goodies like small toys, stickers, or coins if you'd like to trade with other geocachers

Now find a good spot to hide it. You don't want to make it too easy but the fun is in the finding! Be careful to write down the exact coordinates of the GPS so you can add your geocache to the list on geocaching.com.

Happy hunting!

> **DID YOU KNOW?**
>
> The Aldens go geocaching in book #133! In *The Box That Watch Found*, the children stumble across a geocache in the woods. Soon they get their own GPS and start treasure-hunting (and find a mystery too)!

Make a Mini-Museum

During our stay on Surprise Island, we started our own museum to show Grandfather. While on your trip, why not start a collection of memories to share with your friends and family when you get home?

IDEAS TO FILL YOUR MUSEUM CASES:

❏ Postcards of your route

❏ Seashells

❏ Photographs

❏ Sketches of wildlife or your favorite moment during the trip

❏ Souvenirs

❏ Pinecones

❏ Recordings of your voice describing where you are while on your trip and your favorite memory of that place for an interactive exhibit

DESIGNING YOUR MUSEUM

Decide on the space you'll need to show all of your
artifacts, or objects made by humans. You could show
your collection of buttons on a bookcase, put your
artwork in frames on a wall, or share your favorite
postcards on the refrigerator. If you have heavy artifacts,
placing them in boxes on a table is a great way to display
your finds. To be fancy, place the artifact on a piece of
colored fabric to make it stand out.

LABELS

Each artifact should have a small piece of paper near it
saying what the object is and where you found it. Tell
why the piece is special to you and why you chose to
include it in your exhibit.

When your museum is complete, it's time to have
an exhibit opening. Design posters to publicize your
event and invite your friends and family to attend one
afternoon. Don't forget to take pictures to add to the
museum later!

CHAPTER FOUR
The Haunted Boxcar

Halloween is our favorite time of year! We've seen some strange things during our adventures, and even though everything turns out all right, sometimes we wonder if the boxcar may have a little ghost living in it.

When Halloween comes, we love to decorate our boxcar playhouse and Henry likes to tell spooky stories. Violet and Benny love to dress up and I make Benny's favorite creepy sweets.

What was that noise? Okay, the boxcar isn't *really* haunted...is it?

Decorations

SPOOKY LANTERNS

The glow of candlelight is perfect for a spooky night in the boxcar! But instead of using a candle with a real flame, use one that is battery powered to keep you and your home safe from fire.

TO MAKE TISSUE PAPER LANTERNS, YOU WILL NEED:

- ☐ Clear glass votive candleholders or small glass jars (like a baby food jar)
- ☐ Battery-powered tea light candles
- ☐ Tissue paper in your favorite colors
- ☐ Mod Podge craft glue
- ☐ Water
- ☐ Paintbrush

❶ Start by cutting or tearing shapes out of the tissue paper. How about a ghost or a black cat? Cut enough paper to cover the clear surface of the candleholder.

❷ Using your paintbrush, spread a thin layer of Modge Podge on one section of the glass and place your paper on top of the glue. Continue to cover the rest of the glass.

❸ Clean your paintbrush with water so the glue won't dry on the bristles.

❹ When the glue is dry, use your paintbrush to coat one more layer of glue over the paper to seal it, and let dry completely.

❺ After the glue has set, turn on your battery-powered tea light candle and place it inside the holder to see your candle glow!

No tissue paper? Cut out shapes from black construction paper and glue onto the outside of the glass. Be sure to leave spaces between the shapes for the light to shine through. Pop in the battery-powered tea light candle and you're ready to glow!

GLOWING PEEPERS

One night, while coming back from a friend's party, I saw eyes glowing from the bushes! Silly Benny had made these earlier with Henry, and they gave me quite a fright!

YOU WILL NEED:

- ❑ Empty paper towel tubes
- ❑ Glow stick or battery-operated tea light candle
- ❑ Scissors
- ❑ Pencil

To make the peepers, draw a pair of crazy eyes onto the tube and ask an adult to help cut them out. When it gets dark, crack the glow stick to activate the chemicals or turn on the battery-operated tea light candle and place inside the tube. Hide the tubes in the bushes outside, on the doorstep to welcome trick-or-treaters, or use as a night-light for deliciously spooky dreams.

BOO-LLOONS!

These eerie balloons are my favorites! Draw scary faces on white balloons, and then blow them up. Before you tie off the end with a knot, ask an adult to insert an activated glow stick to light up their spooky faces!

GOOGLY-EYED ANCESTORS

Use glue-dots to stick googly eyes onto the eyes of old thrift store photographs! Use as an invitation to a party or frame them without the glass and decorate your house for extra silliness.

THE ALDENS GET SPOOKY!

In *The Pumpkin Head Mystery* (#124), the Boxcar Children have the best job ever—scaring visitors riding the hayride at a local farm! Benny dresses as a skeleton, Violet is a creepy dancing scarecrow, and Jessie is a ghost bride.

Phantom Game

What can be more fun than leaving a secret spooky gift for your friends at Halloween? In the Phantom Game, we leave a basket of goodies such as candy, creepy DVDs, puzzles, my favorite Boxcar Children's book, and Halloween makeup, at the door of two of our favorite friends. I like to include a drawing of a ghost for them to put in a window to show that they've been visited by the phantom. Benny likes to leave the basket with this note on their doorstep before they catch us!

It all started with a little BOO
A knock upon the door and off they flew!

Halloween is almost here, the leaves are flying by
The pumpkins are ripe, there's a witch in the sky!
The Phantom came by the light of the moon
Put him in your window, it's not too soon!

You have been BOO'd!

Choose two families and pass on a treat. Make a copy of the ghost drawing and add it to the bag so they can join in the fun! Put the phantom in the window so others will know you're part of the party!

Happy Halloween!

Tell a Spine-Tingling Ghost Story!

I love to tell stories and the spookier the better! Whether it's late at night around a campfire or at a slumber party with our friends, a story that sends shivers down our spines is the best kind of fun!

When sharing your ghost story, keep these tips in mind to make your friends check under the bed twice before they go to sleep that night. *Jessie Alden*

Is your story going to be creepy or scary?
Gory or silly? A lot of younger kids like stories

that are just a little bit frightening but end with a very good explanation such as a raccoon knocking over the trash can and making all that racket. Older kids like a little more action. Zombies, vampires, and ghosts are great themes to try out—but do they like to bite or just nibble?

To make a truly creepy story, give your characters traits of people you know.
The more familiar your audience is with them, the more likely they'll recognize that something wasn't quite right in that sandwich that their neighbor gave them—it tasted a little bit like toes.

Where you set your story is important too!
Instead of choosing a faraway castle for a story about vampires, how about the mall, school, or the city bus? If your listeners can imagine themselves in the story, they'll enjoy the tale even more.

What the characters do is called the *plot*.
It's no use having a zombie and a victim if they just stare at each other for a few minutes and then go home. Give your main character a problem to figure out. Is she alone in the woods? What was that scraping noise behind her? And what's that smell?

Take an ordinary situation—like walking home from the library on Halloween—and make it sinister.
Describe how the wind feels against your face, how you'd planned the perfect costume—and

how you forgot to double knot your shoelaces so you hoped zombies wouldn't chase you before you made it to your living room. Of course, zombies will be waiting at the playground—they love the slides—so you need to tell how your main character either escapes the undead or becomes a tasty snack.

To tell your story to a group, have them sit close to you.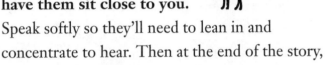
Speak softly so they'll need to lean in and concentrate to hear. Then at the end of the story, yell out the ending to end with a bang!

The secret of any good ghost story is a partner.
Before the story begins, share your tale with a friend and at an agreed-upon point in the tale, have him grab the person sitting next to him.

Every good story needs a good ending.
With a scary story, you want your listeners to react with a jump, a scream, or a good laugh if it's funny. Practice your story before sharing it with your friends. Speak slowly and softly to set the scene and then quickly and franticly at the scary parts to keep your friends on the edge of their seats. If it's a really scary story, you'll want them under their seats.

STORY IDEAS:

Ghost on the teeter-totter

A neighbor with a suspiciously large rose bush that sprang up overnight

A new kid in class that no one else sees but you

A voice in your room

Your reflection in the mirror smiles when you don't

How to make a tombstone rubbing

Cemetery art can be beautiful. Carved angels, flowers, hands, and even skulls decorate many old tombstones and they make a lovely art project to take home to share with your friends by using a technique called tombstone rubbing.

YOU WILL NEED:

- ☐ Plain white paper
- ☐ Dark colored crayon
- ☐ Masking tape (do not use clear tape)
- ☐ Soft brush for cleaning the stone
- ☐ Filled water bottle for cleaning the stones
- ☐ Rag
- ☐ Camera

Before you start your project, please get permission first. Some cemeteries do not allow tombstone rubbings because if it is done incorrectly, it may damage the stones.

After arriving at the cemetery, choose a tombstone that is in good condition with no cracks and doesn't look like it's been repaired in the past. If the stone is in fragile condition, take a photograph instead.

Look for a stone with nice deep carvings so they will show up well in your rubbing. Some cemetery symbols to look for are:

❑   Angels: a guide to heaven

❑   Beehive: home and education

❑   Birds: a symbol of peace

❑   Broken flower: a very young person

❑   Butterfly: resurrection

❑   Circle: everlasting life because there is no beginning or end

❑   Hand pointing down: God descended from Heaven

❑   Hand pointing up: hope of Heaven

❑   Handshake: friendship

❑   Roses: love

❑   Skull and crossbones: death and mortality

❑   Tree trunk: a life cut short

❑   Weeping willow tree: sadness and mourning

LET'S GET STARTED!

❶ To begin your project, see if the stone needs sprucing up. Using the brush, gently sweep away any dirt or mossy lichen attached to the section of stone you'd like to rub. If more cleaning is necessary, spray a small amount of water onto the stone and rub it off with the rag.

❷ Tape the paper over the carving you'd like to copy with masking tape. For larger stones, bring a roll of paper to fit over the stone and tape it to the back of the stone.

❸ Remove the paper wrapper from the crayon and hold the crayon sideways against the stone. With the side of your crayon, begin to gently rub the paper from the outer sections in toward the middle.

❹ When you are finished with the rubbing, remove the tape and admire your handiwork.

Unsolved Mysteries: Wee Beasties

While I believe there is an answer for everything, these creatures are a tough nut to crack! I think we may have our next mystery! Keep your camera ready for a monster mug shot if you run across these creepy critters.

RELEASE THE KRAKEN!

Sounds much more dramatic than "Release the giant squid-thing with lots of arms and a bad attitude!" doesn't it? Up until the mid-nineteenth century, those who braved the seas did so with just a little shiver in their timbers when faced with the prospect of a horrible monster called the kraken. When not attacking ships, the kraken is believed to have epic wrestling matches against sperm whales in the murky depths of the ocean. The whales were later found to have huge sucker marks on

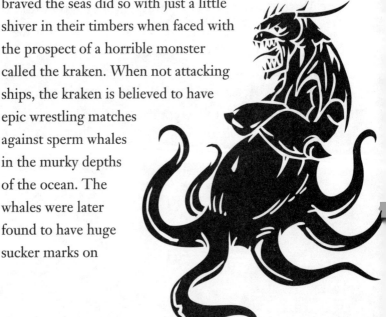

their skin after the battle, much like what's left on your cheek after your aunt comes over on Thanksgiving.

Occasionally, the kraken will surface and be mistaken for a small island. Reports of sailors in the rough North Sea docking their boats and building fires on its slimy surface rarely ended well. As soon as the kraken got a whiff of barbecued squid, it would dive under the cooling waves and drag the unlucky men and their boat to certain death under the sea.

BUNYIP (ALSO KNOWN AS A KIANPRATY)

Haunting the waterways of Australia since the Aboriginal Dreamtime, the mysterious bunyip has warned humans away from its habitat with frightening shrieks. A shape-shifter, the bunyip has been sighted as a starfish as well

HAUNTINGS, HAUNTINGS EVERYWHERE!

Over the course of more than a hundred books, the Boxcar Children have visited a *lot* of places that are rumored to be haunted! Here are just a few:
- The theater in *Ghost in the First Row* (#112), where props mysteriously vanish, and a popcorn-eating spirit has her very own seat.
- In *The Radio Mystery* (#97), the studio of WCXZ is said to be haunted by the ghost of an old-time radio actress!
- *The Ghost at the Drive-In Movie* (#116) features a floating specter that appears late at night and plays strange tricks on moviegoers.

as having feathers or crocodile scales. The most recent reports of the beastie describe it as having a horselike tail and flippers and tusks much like a walrus. Well, I'm glad we cleared that up.

Ancient reports of the bunyip tell of its aggressive nature to defend its soggy territory, devouring anyone who came close enough to poke it with a stick. More modern accounts describe it as more like a grazing, lazy sea cow. European settlers in the mid-nineteenth century stumbling upon the bunyip told of two descriptions of the beast: one with a long, shaggy coat and a doglike face while the other had a long-maned neck to blend with its unkempt coat.

KAPPA

One cranky mutant turtle, the kappa of Japan is unfailingly polite—well, polite until it tries to bite your face off. Found swimming around streams and ponds, the kappa has the unusual feature of a lily pad–shaped bowl or *sara* embedded on the top of its head. The sara is filled with water and is the creature's greatest weakness. If the water spills from the bowl, the

kappa drops to the ground and is helpless until the bowl is refilled. To escape the kappa, bow to it. Its natural tendency to respond in kind will force the creature to bow its head and spill the water.

Recognized for its fierce and mischievous nature, the kappa has been known to attack livestock and at other times pass gas so loudly it's blamed on thunder. The kappa has a fondness for cucumbers so when approaching it, offer a handful of the fruit with your name carved into it for protection. Be warned, the kappa may like you so much that it follows you everywhere—though taking it to the mall may result in fines due to its playing in the fountain and rampaging the food court.

THE BIG GREY MAN OF BEN MACDHUI (OR AM FEAR LIATH MÒR)

This monster is so big, he brings his own climate. Shrouded in the mist of the Cairngorm mountain range in Scotland, the Big Grey Man stalks hikers that dare enter his domain, the peak of Ben MacDhui. Similar to the North American Sasquatch, the Big Grey Man has a reported height of ten to twenty feet and is covered in short brown or gray hair and has feet with toes like talons. The Big Grey Man brings with him his own shroud of fog.

The Big Grey Man might be considered friendly as he often waves his long arms in greeting accompanied with a high-pitched humming sound. However, when meeting the giant, hikers to the region report feelings of doom overtaking them, making them turn and run from the mountain range and to safer areas. Some reports of dark blurs blocking the sky caution that taking a photograph of the Big Grey Man may result in only a foggy shadow. It's difficult to tell if your monster is smiling when his head is in a cloud.

DULLAHAN

Heads up! Washington Irving made Ireland's original headless horseman famous in the United States with the short story, *The Legend of Sleepy Hollow*. Irving's horseman was pretty tough but the dullahan of Irish counties Sligo and Down rides with a glowing head the color of moldy cheese beneath his arm or strapped to his saddle, the head's eyes roll wildly in their sockets, and a wide grin splits its rotting cheeks. When the Dullahan stops his midnight-hued horse outside a household, the head speaks a name—the name of the chosen person. That person's soul is whisked away to become the possession of the Dullahan while the horse's hooves spark against the ground and flames erupt from his steed's nostrils as they speed to the next name on their horrid list.

In other parts of the country, the Dullahan drives a black coach called a coach-a-bower pulled by six black horses. A shrieking banshee may accompany him on his ride, though I can think of better first dates. There is no escape from the Dullahan unless you carry a piece of gold with you at all times as he's afraid of the shiny metal. I'm glad we've never run into the Dullahan on our adventures!

MONSTERS AND MORE!

A list of just some of the supernatural creatures the Aldens have dealt with over the course of the books:

vampire

zombie

gargoyle

walking skeleton

ghost dog

ghost horse

ghost alligator

ghost with a pumpkin for a head

Ogopogo, the Lake Monster!

CHAPTER FIVE
Benny's Belly

Benny's belly can sure get rumbly! I love to cook for my family, and with these easy recipes, you can too! Always have an adult present to help with hot pans or sharp knives and be sure to save me a piece.

Jessie Alden

Breakfast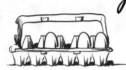

SCRAMBLED EGGS

So quick and easy! We love to add cheese and vegetables to our eggs in the morning for a great start to the day.

INGREDIENTS

1 OR 2 EGGS PER PERSON	DASH OF SALT AND PEPPER
1 TABLESPOON MILK	½ TABLESPOON BUTTER

STEP 1

Melt the butter in a medium-hot pan until it bubbles. Crack the eggs into a bowl and add the salt, pepper, and milk. Beat the mixture together with a fork or a whisk, and add the eggs to the pan. If adding cheese or vegetables, add those now.

STEP 2

Push the eggs from the edges toward the middle while they cook until they are firm.

PANCAKES

Mmmm, pancakes. Perfect with just a little butter and fresh berries on top!

INGREDIENTS

I CUP FLOUR

I TABLESPOON SUGAR

2 TABLESPOONS
  MELTED BUTTER

I TABLESPOON OF
  BAKING POWDER

¾ CUP MILK

I EGG

Mix ingredients together and pour ½ cup at a time onto a buttered griddle. When the pancakes start to bubble on top, flip them over until both sides are golden brown.

GRANOLA

So good in your breakfast bowl, try granola as a topping for ice cream too!

INGREDIENTS

6 CUPS OATS
  (NOT QUICK OATS)

¾ CUP HONEY

¾ CUP VEGETABLE OIL

2 TEASPOON VANILLA

NUTMEG

PUMPKIN PIE SPICE

Preheat oven to 300 degrees, and mix ingredients in a high-sided pan. Bake for 30 minutes, turning oats every ten minutes. Remove from oven when the dinger goes crazy, and stir one more time so the granola doesn't harden, then let cool.

VARIATIONS:

Chocolate granola: Add two tablespoons of cocoa powder to oat mixture before baking, and stir in well.

Chocolate chip granola: Let granola cool in the pan for five minutes, and then stir in handfuls of chocolate chips.

BLUEBERRIES AND CREAM

For dessert or breakfast, I love the little zing of a fresh blueberry!

INGREDIENTS

½ CUP FRESH CHILLED BLUEBERRIES
CREAM

Place blueberries in a bowl, and cover with cold cream.

Lunch

EGG SALAD

Aunt Jane made the best egg salad for lunchtime! I love mine on toasted multigrain bread for a little extra crunch.

INGREDIENTS

6 BOILED EGGS WITH
  SHELLS REMOVED
1 TABLESPOON MUSTARD
2 TABLESPOONS MAYONNAISE

PINCH OF SALT
PINCH OF PEPPER
MULTIGRAIN BREAD
  FOR SANDWICH

STEP 1

Place eggs in a pan, and cover with cold water. With help from an adult, heat the uncovered pan on the stove until the water is boiling, and then turn off the heat, and cover the pan with a lid. Wait 15 minutes for large eggs and 20 minutes for extra-large eggs. Ask an adult to drain the pan into the sink to remove the hot water, and run cold water over the eggs until they are cool enough to handle.

STEP 2

Peel the shells off the eggs. Add eggs to a medium-sized bowl, and smash with a fork into small pieces.

STEP 3

Add mustard, mayonnaise, salt, and pepper to the eggs, and mix.

STEP 4

Add a thin layer of mayonnaise to one side of bread slices, and scoop egg salad onto the bread to make a delicious sandwich.

PIZZA

Forget store-bought pizza. With this pie, the fun is in the dough! Have a contest with everyone making his or her own small pizza and share a bite to see whose pizza you like best. Give points for extra creativity. I love sausage, mushrooms, olives, and salty sardines—what about you?

INGREDIENTS

I PACKAGE DRY YEAST	I TABLESPOON OLIVE OIL
¾ CUP WARM WATER	2 CUPS FLOUR
PINCH OF SALT	COOKING SPRAY

TOPPINGS

PIZZA SAUCE	PINEAPPLE	SARDINES
PEPPERONI	OLIVES	CHEESE
SAUSAGE	CHICKEN	
MUSHROOMS	VEGGIES	

STEP 1

Mix ¾ cups of warm water with the package of dry yeast in a large bowl. Wait until the yeast is bubbly, then add salt, olive oil, and flour, and stir together. Sprinkle some flour onto a cutting board, and transfer the dough onto the surface. Knead the dough for about five minutes.

BOXCAR TIP If the dough gets a little sticky, **add in a little bit of flour.**

STEP 2

Place the dough into a large bowl that has been coated with cooking spray (so the dough won't stick to the edges). Cover the bowl with plastic wrap, and let it sit in a warm spot for one hour.

STEP 3

Preheat the oven to 400 degrees. Remove your dough from the bowl, and give it a good poke. Roll the dough into a ball, and let it sit for another 15 minutes.

STEP 4

Put a little flour on your hands and flatten the dough onto your pizza pan or parchment-paper-covered cookie sheet. Add toppings and pop into the oven for 25 minutes.

STEP 5

Remove from the oven with help from an adult and let cool. Cut into slices and share with a friend!

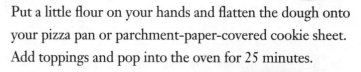

SOME OF BENNY'S FAVORITE FOODS

Pancakes   Hamburgers   Granola Bars
Hot dogs   Popcorn

Supper

HOT DOGS IN A MILK CARTON

When we camp, we love this fun way to cook hot dogs in
an empty carton. Be sure to have an adult present at all
times while around the campfire!

INGREDIENTS

HOT DOG

BUN

CLEAN HALF-GALLON MILK
  CARTON WITH PLASTIC
  POUR SPOUT REMOVED

NEWSPAPER

TIN FOIL

STEP 1

Place the hot dog in the bun, and roll it up in a square of
tin foil. Place the hot dog into the milk carton, and stuff
the remaining space with crumpled newspapers.

STEP 2

Have an adult place the carton in the coals of your
campfire, and wait for the carton to completely burn away.

STEP 3

Ask an adult to remove the hot dog from the campfire,
and unwrap your hot dog. Add your favorite toppings,
and enjoy!

CLAM CHOWDER

This recipe was so good on Surprise Island!

INGREDIENTS

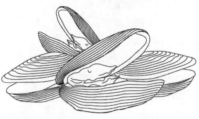

I SLICE BACON, DICED

I SMALL ONION, CHOPPED

I CUP PEELED
  CUBED POTATOES

2 CUPS WATER

I CAN (6½ OUNCES)
  MINCED CLAMS

2 CUPS MILK

3 TABLESPOONS
  MELTED BUTTER

2 TABLESPOONS FLOUR

½ TEASPOON SALT

¼ TEASPOON PEPPER

STEP 1

Fry bacon until crispy.

STEP 2

Add onion to the bacon, and cook until soft.

STEP 3

Add potatoes and water. Bring the water to a boil, then turn down the heat, and cook until the potatoes are soft when you poke them.

STEP 4

Add clams and milk, and cook for five minutes.

STEP 5

In bowl, mix melted butter, flour, salt, and pepper together. Slowly add to the chowder, stirring until the chowder thickens and is ready to enjoy.

Desserts

Benny's favorite meal!

APRIL FOOLS' PIE

This may taste like apple pie, but it isn't!

INGREDIENTS

2 CUPS WATER

2 CUPS SUGAR

2 TEASPOONS CREAM OF TARTAR

2 UNBAKED PIE SHELLS

36 TO 40 RITZ CRACKERS

LEMON ZEST (SCRAPE THE
OUTSIDE OF A LEMON RIND)

2 TABLESPOONS LEMON JUICE

I TEASPOON CINNAMON

¼ TEASPOON NUTMEG

2 TABLESPOONS OF BUTTER
CUT INTO SMALL PIECES

STEP 1

Preheat oven to 350 degrees.

STEP 2

In a small saucepan, heat the water, sugar, and cream of tartar until it reaches a boil.

STEP 3

Add the lemon juice and lemon zest to the syrup. Reduce the heat to low, and simmer (just before a boil) for 15 minutes.

STEP 4

Remove the syrup from the heat, and allow it to cool slightly.

STEP 5

Place one piecrust in a pie tin. Crumble the crackers into the pie shell. Pour the syrup over the crackers, and dust the cinnamon and nutmeg over the mixture. Cover the pie with the remaining piecrust. Pinch the edges together, and make two small cuts in the top piecrust to vent.

STEP 6

Bake the pie for 30 to 35 minutes or until crust is golden brown. Remove from the oven and let cool.

MARY'S CHERRY DUMPLINGS

Mary makes the most delicious cherry dumplings!

INGREDIENTS

CHERRY PIE FILLING

REFRIGERATED PIECRUST
DOUGH OR CROISSANT
DOUGH

STEP 1

Preheat oven to temperature listed on the dough packaging.

STEP 2

Roll out the dough into a large circle on a floured surface. Use a rolling pin or large jar to make it flat.

STEP 3

Cut circles out of the dough by using a large round cookie cutter or the mouth of a jar or glass.

STEP 4

Spoon cherry pie filling into the center of the dough, and then fold the dough over to make a pretty half-moon, and pinch the edges to close it up tight

STEP 5

Place your dumplings onto a parchment-paper covered cookie sheet, and bake for the time recommended on the dough packaging or until the crust is a nice golden color. Enjoy!

PEACH COBBLER

Grandfather's favorite dish. He likes to eat it with homemade ice cream too!

INGREDIENTS

I CUP SUGAR

I CUP FLOUR

I CUP MILK

I TABLESPOON
  BAKING POWDER

I QUART CANNED DICED
  PEACHES

I TABLESPOON BUTTER

STEP 1

Preheat the oven to 425 degrees. Melt the butter in a 9 x 11 baking dish in the warming oven.

STEP 2

In a bowl, combine the sugar, flour, milk, and baking powder with a large mixer.

STEP 3

Drain fruit, and then heat it to boiling in a saucepan.

STEP 4

When the fruit is ready, remove the baking dish from the oven, and pour the batter over the butter. Spoon the fruit over the batter.

STEP 5

Bake for 15 to 20 minutes, then remove from the oven, and let cool before serving.

ICE CREAM IN A BAG

Violet loves homemade ice cream, and by making it this way she can have it in no time!

INGREDIENTS

1 PINT-SIZED ZIPPERED PLASTIC BAG
1 GALLON-SIZED ZIPPERED PLASTIC BAG
ICE CUBES
1 CUP HALF-AND-HALF
½ CUP ROCK SALT OR KOSHER SALT

2 TABLESPOONS OF SUGAR
½ TEASPOON VANILLA EXTRACT
YOUR FAVORITE MIX-INS: CHOCOLATE SYRUP, FRUIT, COCONUT, ETC.

STEP 1

In the pint-sized (smaller) bag, combine the sugar, half-and-half, and vanilla. Seal it up tight!

STEP 2

Put the smaller bag into the larger zippered bag, and fill the rest of the bag with ice cubes and the salt. Get your wiggle on and shake the bags for at least five minutes. The crazier the dance moves, the better.

STEP 3

When the inner bag is as firm as you like it, remove it from the bigger bag, and rinse it under water to remove any salt from the outside. Add your mix-ins, and enjoy it right out of the bag!

Drinks

What's a meal without a frosty drink? Make your own lemonade and eggnog to share with these easy recipes.

LEMONADE

INGREDIENTS

6 LEMONS

I CUP SUGAR

6 CUPS COLD WATER

ICE CUBES

STEP 1

Roll the lemons under your hands on a hard surface until squishy. Cut the lemons in half, and squeeze the juice into a pitcher. Be careful not to add any seeds for extra pucker power.

STEP 2

Combine the lemon juice, sugar, and water in the pitcher, and stir until the sugar is dissolved. Add ice. Find a good book and a shady tree. Read until suppertime.

EGGNOG

INGREDIENTS

1 EGG

2 TABLESPOONS SUGAR

1 CUP COLD MILK

¼ TEASPOON VANILLA

1 DASH NUTMEG

STEP 1

With an adult, whisk the egg, sugar, and milk in a heated saucepan.

STEP 2

Cook over medium heat until the egg begins to stick to the whisk or begins to steam. Stir constantly—do not allow the nog to boil or it may curdle.

STEP 3

Stir in the vanilla.

STEP 4

Pour mixture into a glass or bowl, and place into the refrigerator to cool. Before serving, stir it again with the whisk, and add the dash of nutmeg.

CHAPTER SIX
Violet's Workbag

GREAT DIY BOXCAR CHILDREN MOMENTS

The Aldens can be mighty handy when it comes to projects! Here's a few examples...

The Mystery at the Fair (special #6): Jessie and her friend Courtney make African bead earrings for the county fair and win a prize!

The Boardwalk Mystery (#131): When the owner of Hanson's Amusement Pier needs help advertising, Violet designs a T-shirt for the Aldens to wear on the boardwalk.

Snowbound Mystery (#13): Oh no, squirrels are running loose in the attic of the Aldens' cabin! But Henry and Benny build a clever trap to catch them safely and let them go.

Violet always has a project going! What's in your busy bag for a crafty day?

Jessie Alden

How to Make a Silhouette

Before photographs were quick and easy, people cut out outlines of their friends, called *silhouettes*, to remember them by. Follow these steps to make your own.

❶ Have a friend sit sideways in a chair a few feet from a wall.

❷ Using a projector or a lamp with its shade removed, shine the light so that you can see her profile against the wall.

❸ Tape a piece of black construction paper to the wall where the shadow falls. You may need to move the projector closer or farther away for the shadow to fit well.

❹ With a white crayon or piece of chalk, carefully outline the shadow onto the black paper.

❺ When you're finished tracing, remove the black paper from the wall and cut out the silhouette.

❻ Glue the black paper onto a lighter colored paper and frame. Now try it with your family for an art show!

Pressing Flowers

Violet and I love to press flowers for craft projects. We use flowers that are in bloom in our backyard or wildflowers. Be sure to ask permission from an adult if you are not picking flowers from your own yard.

TO MAKE YOUR PRESS:

❶ Gather your flowers or leaves. Choose flowers that have a naturally flat heads like daisies. Pick the flowers in the morning, right after they bloom, and dry off as much dew as possible before you press them. Larger-headed flowers, such as roses or carnations, will take longer to dry.

❷ Place your flowers in the refrigerator so they won't wilt while you gather your supplies:

- ☐ newspaper (or 6 to 8 sheets of paper)
- ☐ dictionary or other heavy books

TO PRESS THE FLOWERS:

❶ Open the newspaper to the center, and place your flowers onto the newsprint. Fold the paper over to cover the flowers completely. If you're using sheets of paper, place the flowers between 3 or 4 sheets and cover with 3 or 4 more sheets. Make sure the flowers do not overlap.

❷ Open your heavy book to the center and tuck the papers between the sheets. If you're using a dictionary, look for the M section. Place more books on top to weigh down the pages.

❸ After three days, remove the papers and check to see if your flowers are completely dry and squished. It may take up to a week for the flowers to dry though the squishing part is much quicker.

CRAFTS USING PRESSED FLOWERS:

❶ Cut two large pieces of packing tape. Place your flowers on one piece and carefully place the other piece on top of the flowers. Cut away the extra tape in a fun shape around the flower. Using a hole puncher, make a hole near the top and thread a ribbon. Knot the ribbon at the ends to make a lovely necklace or sun catcher for your window.

❷ Cut a narrow strip of construction paper about 4 inches long. Glue your pressed flower to the paper and cover with packing tape for a great bookmark to give as a gift or keep your place in your favorite Boxcar Children's book!

❸ Use Mod Podge to glue flowers onto eggshells. To keep the shell and not the egg, ask your mom or dad to help you blow out the egg inside by using two pinpricks on either end of the egg, one smaller than the other. Over the sink, blow into the small hole so the egg leaves the shell through the larger hole. After all of the egg is gone, rinse and dry the shell, and then apply the flowers. After the glue is dry, cover with a thin coat of Mod Podge to seal.

Yarn Octopus Doll

Benny made an octopus for his stuffed bear. I think they make great friends!

YOU WILL NEED:

- ❑ 2 inch Styrofoam ball or a small baby sock filled with polyfill
- ❑ 1 skein of yarn
- ❑ scissors
- ❑ black marker or 2 large googly eyes
- ❑ 1 gallon milk jug, empty

HOW TO MAKE THE OCTOPUS:

❶ Cut off two pieces of yarn about six inches long and set aside.

❷ Take the rest of the yarn and wind it around the base of the milk jug until you have used up the entire skein. Then slide the yarn off the jug. You should now have a ring of yarn. Tie one of the pieces of yarn from Step 1 around the middle of the ring and knot it tightly.

❸ Place the ball or stuffed sock directly under the knot you have just made. Wrap the yarn over the ball or sock until it is covered. This will be the "head," and the knot will be on top. Tie the remaining piece of yarn from Step 1 under the "head" on the opposite side of the first knot.

❹ The yarn at the bottom will still be in a loop. Cut through the loop so that all the strands of yarn hang free.

❺ Divide the yarn strands into eight sections. These will be the "tentacles." (You may want to count the strands of yarn to make sure each section is even.) Braid each section and tie off each end with a piece of yarn or colorful ribbon to complete each tentacle.

❻ Glue the googly eyes onto the head or make eyeballs with the black marker.

A Thauma-what?

Henry would make these simple animation toys, called a *thaumatrope*, while we were staying in our little boxcar. By drawing a picture on one side and its opposite on the other, they flipped so fast that it fooled the eye into thinking it was moving!

YOU WILL NEED:
- one piece of thin cardboard (like from a cereal box) or heavy card stock
- small plate
- pencil
- scissors
- hole punch
- two rubber bands
- crayons or pictures cut from a magazine

TO MAKE YOUR THAUMATROPE:

❶ Using the small plate and the pencil, trace a circle onto the cardboard.

❷ Cut out the circle.

❸ Draw a picture such as a bumblebee or bird with its wings up on one side of the circle and its wings down on the other side. How about a fish on one side and the bowl on the other? If you're using magazine photos, have one person talking to another—just make sure they're on opposite sides of the circle.

❹ Use the hole punch to make holes on either side of the circle.

❺ Loop a rubber band into each hole.

❻ While holding the rubber bands in each hand, ask a friend to wind the thaumatrope up like a paddle on a toy boat. After it's wound up, pull on the rubber bands so that it spins. Watch as the pictures become one! To keep it spinning, bring your hands close together and then far apart while it rotates.

Jungle in a Jar

Making a terrarium is a fantastic way to have a garden right in your room. A terrarium is like a tiny greenhouse by using sunlight to warm the soil, plants, and air through the clear glass of its jar. It creates its own climate by using that sunlight to heat up the moisture in the soil, and through evaporation and condensation can keep the plants watered and happy.

To begin your terrarium, decide on what plants you'd like to use. Succulents, like cactus, require very little watering and need a wide-mouthed jar like a goldfish bowl. Plants that like the weather a little stickier, such as ferns and begonias, do well in a closed container like a cookie jar or glass pickle jar with a lid.

SUPPLIES YOU WILL NEED:

- ❏ container: clear glass is best to let the sunlight in
- ❏ rocks: marble-sized or smaller
- ❏ activated charcoal (found at pet stores)
- ❏ potting soil
- ❏ small plants

OPTIONAL:

- ❏ seashells
- ❏ twigs
- ❏ moss

INSTRUCTIONS:

❶ Fill your jar with a 1-inch layer of rocks. This helps the soil drain and the plants' roots to stay healthy.

❷ Sprinkle ½-inch of charcoal over the soil.

❸ Fill the jar halfway full of potting soil

❹ Make a small hole in the soil. Remove your plants from their containers and gently place them inside the hole in the terrarium. Pat a little soil under the plant to keep the roots protected.

❺ Add decorative pebbles, moss, or plastic dinosaurs to give your terrarium a little personality.

❻ Give your plants a little water. If you're using a closed container, place the lid. Set your terrarium in indirect sunlight and watch your plants grow.

BOXCAR TIP

If you are using a lid on your terrarium, you will see condensation form on the inside of the jar. This is how the plants water themselves. Be careful of watering the plants too much in the beginning, however, since root rot can set in. If there is too much condensation, remove the lid for an hour and replace later.

CHAPTER SEVEN
A Friend in Need

Be sure not to let the dog off the leash!

THE BOXCAR CHILDREN'S RESUME!

A *resume* is a list of places where someone has worked. Henry, Jessie, Violet, and Benny have worked at so many places, the list is probably a mile long, but here are some highlights:

Greenfield Museum

bookstore

horse ranch

amusement park

shopping mall

reality TV show

Iowa corn maze

pizza restaurant

radio station

ice cream parlor

When the Aldens see a problem, we always pitch in to help. What can you do to help your community and have fun at the same time? Having a job doesn't always mean wearing a suit and tie or driving to a big office. We can do things at every age to get the job done!

WRITER

Do you find yourself wishing you had broken the story about the dog trapped in the abandoned house and fooling the neighborhood into thinking there was a ghost with its howls? As a writer, you share information through your stories either for entertainment or to share news. Start a neighborhood newsletter! Include news from around your area with photos, interviews of your friends and neighbors, and keep everyone in the know.

Love the Internet? With permission from your parents, start a blog and write down the stories in your head. Upload pictures you've drawn yourself to accompany the story and you'll have a book in no time.

PET SITTER AND DOG WALKING

When friends and family go on vacation, some furry or scaly family members need a cuddle and some exercise when left at home. When advertising your pet sitting services, ask an adult to print out a flyer with your prices and how to contact you. Only give the flyers to people you know and make sure you go with a friend or an adult when you are on the job in case you need help.

BABYSITTING AND PARENT HELPER

Sometimes a parent needs a hand when children are underfoot. As a babysitter, you'll be watching the children when parents are away, while as a parent helper, you help out when a parent is at home. Both jobs require patience, creativity, and a knack for having fun! If the parent is leaving the house, make sure you write down all important information, such as their cell phone numbers, what time they'll be home, house rules, and any allergy information in case of emergency.

A great babysitter and helper always has a plan before she arrives. Bring along stickers, books, and your favorite board games for indoors or head outside for a game of zombie tag or a scavenger hunt. Stuck for ideas? Turn on some music for a dance party and get those wiggles out!

Before starting their babysitting businesses, kids ages 11 to 15 should consider taking a babysitting course from the American Red Cross to be prepared for emergencies.

FAMILY BUSINESS

Does your parent work from home? Ask to help him or her with office work such as filing, copying papers, or picking up the mail.

YARD WORK

Grab a rake and some friends and get busy chasing leaves! Ask a neighbor if you can help them by picking up branches or raking the leaves in autumn to help keep your street tidy. In the spring, lend a hand by helping plant flowers, and in the summer, weed the flowerbeds. Be on the lookout for small animals, they love to hide under bushes!

VOLUNTEERING

There are many fun and exciting projects in your community that need help. The local animal shelter may need blankets and food for pets before they find their forever homes, and many retirement home residents would love to spend time talking or doing crafts with kids. How about a bake sale or lemonade stand to earn money to help a local food bank? Pitch in and get your hands dirty in a neighborhood garden to help those who need a little extra help at the dinner table. Volunteering makes you feel great!

CHAPTER EIGHT
Games

SIX GAME-TASTIC BOXCAR CHILDREN MYSTERIES

Whether participating in a scavenger hunt, a word-making challenge, or just solving a riddle, the Aldens love games. Here's a few books about them:

#118, *The Spy Game*

#115, *The Great Detective Race*

#104, *The Game Store Mystery*

#87, *The Mystery of the Spider's Clue*

#Special 10, *The Windy City Mystery*

When not solving mysteries, we love to play games! Benny likes to play games with a group of kids, while Violet loves to play on her own or with only one or two good friends.

When you play a game with friends or family, here are a few tips to keep things fair and everyone happy.

◆　Decide on the rules first. If everyone knows how to play the game and what the rules are, you won't have an argument later. If you'd like to change the rules, wait until next time so you're all on the same page.

◆　Safety first!

◆　Always listen to your coach or the officials.

◆　Play fair and square. Cheaters can ruin a game fast.

◆　Treat the other game players as you'd like them to treat you. That means no mean words.

◆　Can't agree? Sometimes it's better to stop the game and try another if you can't see eye to eye.

◆　Always do your best! It doesn't matter if you lose; you'll have fun trying and can look forward to playing the next game.

◆　Mix the game up a little next time. If you're playing tag, try a version of zombie or freeze tag. If you play Red Rover, have everyone pick a secret color instead of names and try to guess it so they can join you!

◆　Are you playing on a team? Before the game, make up a cheer to yell and get everyone in the spirit!

◆ Even if you're super good with the ball or can double Dutch until the cows come home, try not to show off.

◆ Taking turns is important in games with a lot of people. When it's your turn to sit on the sidelines, don't forget to cheer on your teammates!

◆ Be a good friend. If your team loses, don't make excuses or pin the blame on one particular person. Mistakes are the way we learn and that includes learning new sportsmanship skills.

◆ Losing a game can be hard but it's part of the learning process. Next time, you'll be able to try a new approach or watch and pick up tips from your teammates to try when your turn is up.

◆ Be a gracious winner. A smile and a handshake is a great way to make a new friend after the game.

◆ When you win, shake the other players' hands.

◆ When you lose, shake the other players' hands.

◆ Say thank you to your coaches and referees. They love the game as much as you do but they don't get to play!

Phew! Those are a lot of things to go over but now we're ready to check out the games. Where do we start first? Group games? Indoors or out? Let's go!

Games to play outdoors

Nothing's better than sharing a game with your friends under a bright blue sky. Try these games on the playground or in a space with lots of room to run.

TAG

Who's *it*? This fast-paced game is fun for everyone and picks up extra players in a jiffy, so be quick—it looks like it's your turn!

How to play: Run like crazy until you're tagged as *it*, then tag another player

To start a game: Players yell "Not it!" The last to shout it out is *it*. Players scatter and *it* chases the players until tagging the next *it*.

Number of players: Any number but the bigger the better.

Ages: All ages but keep an eye out for smaller players.

Where to play: Tag can be played anywhere there is space to run, but a large field or grassy area is best in case you get knocked down.

Equipment needed: Feet

Base: Choose a safe base for players to take a breather, like a tree, a chair, a mom…

MIXING IT UP:
DIFFERENT WAYS TO PLAY TAG

Touch tag: When *it* touches another player, that player becomes *it*. Run, run, run!

Touch tag variation: After *it* touches another player, they both become *it* and chase the others until no more players are left. The last player tagged becomes *it* in the next game.

Shadow tag: While playing basic tag, players can tag others by stepping on their shadows instead of touching them. Excellent for after-school games of tag or under a full moon so that your shadows are longer.

Band-aid tag: When *it* tags another player, that player must hold onto the place where he was tagged or "injured." If he's tagged again, he must hold onto that spot as well as the first. If tagged three times, the player must go to the "hospital" on the sidelines and do five jumping jacks before returning to the game.

Freeze tag: When *it* tags a player, that player must freeze in position and remain there until another player "melts" her by touching her and she is able to rejoin the game. If *it* sees the frozen player move before she's melted, the player is then called out as *it*. If *it* catches another player trying to melt a frozen player, the "melter" becomes *it*. If a player is frozen three times, she must run to the sidelines and do five jumping jacks before returning to the game to keep her warmed up!

Flashlight tag: Playing tag at night takes special skills, so grab a flashlight and get ready to run! To play, *it* must shine his flashlight beam onto a player to tag her. The flashlight then changes hands and everyone scatters! Adults love this game too so get your parents into the chase!

Blob tag: After being tagged by *it*, the player holds hands or links elbows with *it* and runs with her to tag the next player. Each player who gets tagged joins the "blob." The wigglier the blob, the better!

Tunnel tag: Just like in freeze tag, the player must freeze when touched by *it*. To melt him, another player must squeeze through the frozen player's legs for him to rejoin the game.

Zombie tag: A slower-moving game of tag if you're *it*, this version requires *it* to move with stiff legs and outstretched arms like a zombie. Groaning is encouraged. The other players must get as close to the zombie *it* as possible without *it* lunging for them and tagging them as the new *it*.

Zombie tag variation: After *it* tags a person, she too becomes a zombie and chases the others until all players have been infected. The last player tagged becomes the new *it*.

Time warp tag: During the game, *it* can call out "Time warp!" and all players must slow down and run in slow motion until *it* calls out "Time warp!" again and everyone can return to their usual crazy fast speed.

Blind man's bluff: You'll need a blindfold to play this variation of tag so whip out your bandana and cover those peepers. To play, *it* has his eyes covered and the other players turn him in a circle three times. *It* then tries to tag players while unable to see. This game is best with a small group so the game moves quickly.

Tip: Make sure the area is safe from things to trip on or holes to fall into. We want everyone to be safe and have a great time.

Fainting goat tag: *It* becomes the goatherd for the flock of fainting goats. A player (goat) may avoid being tagged by dropping to the ground for ten seconds before running away. The goats cannot fall to the ground unless the goatherd is closer than ten feet from them.

MARBLES

How to play: Draw a circle about six feet in diameter with chalk or in the dirt with a stick. Players attempt to knock each other's marbles out of the circle by using a shooter marble. Each player drops his or her marbles within the circle. Agree upon the person to go first.

The shooter marble must stay within the circle. If it rolls outside of the circle or you fail to hit another marble, your turn is over. If the shooter marble stops within the circle but doesn't hit another player's marble, it stays put until your next turn.

If you hit another player's marble, you may go again from wherever your shooter marble is within the circle

When the circle is empty, the player with the most marbles wins!

Number of players: 2–6

Ages: Keep marbles out of the hands of little ones as they may become a choking hazard

Where to play: Outside on a flat surface of concrete or dirt

Equipment needed: At least 6 marbles

BOXCAR TIP

Some marbles champs play for keeps, so make sure you know the ground rules before you start playing. If you don't want to part with your marbles (or if you don't want to keep the other players' marbles) after the game, make sure everyone is on the same page.

HIDE-AND-SEEK

How to play: One player is the seeker; the others hide until the seeker finds them. Set boundaries so you're not hiding a mile away while everyone else is playing in the front yard. The seeker closes his or her eyes and counts to twenty while the other players scatter to a hiding place. The game is finished when the seeker finds all of the players or yells "Olly, olly, oxen free!" to signal the end of the game without penalty to the hiders.

Number of players: 2–10

Ages: All ages

Where to play: Indoors and outdoors but stay within the boundaries or you're automatically out!

Equipment needed: Sneaky feet

Variations:

Pick a place to become home base. Hiders may run to base to be "safe" when the seeker isn't looking. If the seeker finds them and tags them before they reach home base, they are out for the rest of the game.

SARDINES

A fun switcheroo on hide-and-seek! Just how many people *can* you get into a boxcar?

How to play: One player becomes the "sardine." The other players cover their eyes and count to fifty while the sardine hides. After the sardine is well hidden, the seekers spread out to find the sardine. If you find him or her, don't say a word! Instead, hide along with the sardine. Soon, most of the seekers will be packed into the space with the sardine until only one seeker is left!

Number of players: 5–15

Ages: All ages

Where to play: A park with a lot of bushes or playground equipment, or inside—just be careful not to knock over things when you're packed in tight.

Equipment needed: Ability to squish together and not make a peep

GHOST

How to play: Three to four players are chosen to be the "ghosts" while the rest of the players pick a spot to stand and close their eyes. The ghosts will haunt a player by standing very quietly behind her without the ghost being noticed and count in his head to ten. If the player does not catch the ghost, the ghost will tap her lightly on the shoulder. The player then sits down and waits quietly for the end of the game.

If a player feels the presence of the ghost, she may ask, "Is there a ghost behind me?" If she is correct, she becomes a ghost as well.

Number of players: 5–50

Ages: All ages

Where to play: Indoors or outdoors depending on number of players

Equipment needed: Spooky feet

CAPTURE THE FLAG

How to play: Each team takes five minutes to hide their flag somewhere on their side of the playing field. When both teams are ready, it's on! Teams cross over the dividing line to find the other team's flag and bring it back to their side.

The first team to bring the opponent's flag to its territory wins!

Number of players: 10 or more players with enough for two equal teams

Ages: All ages

Where to play: A large outdoor area such as a field or *big* backyard. Divide the playing area into two equal sides. Each team has a jail and a home base near the back.

Equipment needed: Two "flags" made of any kind of material

Rules: Tag your opponents when they cross over the line! The tagged players must go to your jail and cannot rejoin the game unless they are tagged back by a member of their team.

If you are tagged on the other side, you must drop the flag where you are tagged and head to jail.

Variations:

Instead of jail, have tagged players join your side against their old teammates for the rest of the game.

Tag players with water balloons or snowballs (gently).

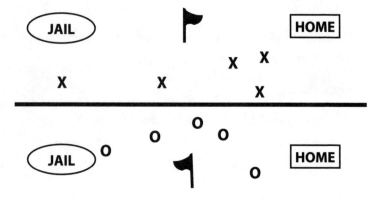

NINJA

A little bit of capture the flag with a dash of ninja action!

How to play: Divide players into two teams, ninjas and guards. The ninja team will have a home base, such as a tree, rock, or super-slick ninja hideout, to return their captured items to, while the guards have a jail. The guards place items on the ground and stand about ten feet away from each item.

Have one player be the head guard. When the game starts, all the guards except for the head guard close their eyes and give the ninjas time to sneak toward an item to snatch it. Every minute or so, the head guard will yell out "Alarm!" and the guards chase after the ninjas as they run back to base. If a guard tags a ninja, the ninja must go to jail until another ninja tags him to set him free.

When all of the ninjas are in jail, the guards win the game. If the ninjas succeed in bringing all the items back to their hideout, they win.

Number of players: Any number

Ages: All ages

Where to play: A large outdoor space. Divide the playing area into two equal sides.

Equipment needed: Items for the ninjas to snatch like a ball, doll, or rock.

SWING THE STATUE

How to play: One player is chosen to be *it*. *It* takes the hand or wrist of another player and swings her in a circle until letting go. The swung player (the statue) will try to remain frozen in place after she's come to a complete stop. The first player to wiggle becomes the next *it*. Don't crack a smile!

Number of players: 2–20

Ages: Any age but be careful of the little ones

Where to play: Outside on a grassy lawn

Equipment needed: Feet and an arm

HOPSCOTCH

How to play: Draw a grid on sidewalk with chalk, or use a stick to scratch the grid into dirt. Number each square. On his turn, a player tosses a stone onto the first square on the grid. The player hops on one foot to the end of the grid, skipping the square with the stone in it. On a double grid, the player must plop both feet in the squares (unless there is a stone in one of the squares). He then hops back to the beginning, picking up the stone on his way back. On the next turn, the player tosses the stone onto the next number and moves up the grid with every turn until he reaches the end.

A player wins by completing the grid without stepping onto a square with both feet or without his stone bouncing out of bounds or sliding into another square.

Number of players: 1 or more

Ages: 7 and up

Where to play: Outside on a flat sidewalk, driveway, or dirt

Equipment needed: Chalk or a stick

Lingo: The stone may also be called a potsy, marker, or puck.

POTSY (NEW YORK HOPSCOTCH)

In this game, a potsy is made out of three paper clips clipped together to form a triangle. After the player completes a full grid, she may choose a square to write her name in with chalk. No other player can hop on that square for the rest of the game.

ESCARGOT

Escargot means "snail" in French, but let's see how fast you can hop through that grid! In France, this version of hopscotch is played with no stone. The player hops through the grid on one foot to the *home* square in the center of the grid (the snail). He may take a rest, then hop back on the same foot to the beginning. If the player makes it back without stepping on both feet, he may choose a square to write his name or initials in. From then on, only that player may step on that square.

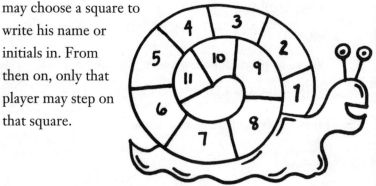

Card Games

Violet loves to challenge Henry to card games when it's raining outside. She always deals an extra hand for Watch since he likes to Go Fish!

GO FISH

How to play: The dealer hands out seven cards to each player, including herself. The rest of the cards are placed facedown between the players to form a "stock." The player to the left of the dealer starts the game by asking another player for a specific type of card such as fours or aces. If the other player has any of those cards, she must give them to the asker. If she does not have any of the cards, the asker draws a card from the stock and the player to her left asks next. If the asker does receive the card or cards she asked for, she may have another turn.

Once a player has a *book* of four cards (hearts, spade, clubs, diamonds), she places them in a pile in front of her on the table. The game continues until no more cards are left to trade. Whoever has the most books wins.

Number of players: 2 or more

Ages: 7 and up

Where to play: Anywhere

Equipment needed: 52-card deck

SLAPJACK

This card game is fast and furious. Be the first to collect all the cards to win by slapping the Jack when he comes up!

How to play: Deal the deck equally between all the players. The players hold their cards facedown and reveal them one at a time in a pile in the center. If a Jack is revealed, the first to slap their hand down on the card collects all of the cards in the pile.

Once a player is out of cards, he is out of the game unless he manages to slap a Jack as the others play. He may then rejoin the game. The player with all of the cards at the end of the game is the winner!

Number of players: 2 or more

Ages: 5 and up

Where to play: Anywhere

Equipment needed: 52-card deck

Conclusion

I hope you had fun with the Boxcar Children Guide to Adventure! Henry, Benny, and Violet sure loved helping me write this book so I hope you try something new and share it with a friend. Remember to stay curious, be respectful of everything and everyone you meet, help where you can, and most of all, be kind. See you at the boxcar!

Jessie Alden

The Boxcar Children Mysteries

The Boxcar Children Mysteries

The Movie Star Mystery
The Mystery of the Pirate's Map
The Ghost Town Mystery
The Mystery of the Black Raven
The Mystery in the Mall
The Mystery in New York
The Gymnastics Mystery
The Poison Frog Mystery
The Mystery of the Empty Safe
The Home Run Mystery
The Great Bicycle Race Mystery
The Mystery of the Wild Ponies
The Mystery in the Computer
  Game
The Mystery at the Crooked
  House
The Hockey Mystery
The Mystery of the Midnight Dog
The Mystery of the Screech Owl
The Summer Camp Mystery
The Copycat Mystery
The Haunted Clock Tower
  Mystery
The Mystery of the Tiger's Eye
The Disappearing Staircase
  Mystery
The Mystery on Blizzard
  Mountain
The Mystery of the Spider's Clue
The Candy Factory Mystery
The Mystery of the Mummy's
  Curse
The Mystery of the Star Ruby
The Stuffed Bear Mystery
The Mystery of Alligator Swamp
The Mystery at Skeleton Point
The Tattletale Mystery
The Comic Book Mystery
The Great Shark Mystery
The Ice Cream Mystery
The Midnight Mystery
The Mystery in the Fortune
  Cookie

The Black Widow Spider Mystery
The Radio Mystery
The Mystery of the Runaway
  Ghost
The Finders Keepers Mystery
The Mystery of the Haunted
  Boxcar
The Clue in the Corn Maze
The Ghost of the Chattering
  Bones
The Sword of the Silver Knight
The Game Store Mystery
The Mystery of the Orphan Train
The Vanishing Passenger
The Giant Yo-Yo Mystery
The Creature in Ogopogo Lake
The Rock 'n' Roll Mystery
The Secret of the Mask
The Seattle Puzzle
The Ghost in the First Row
The Box That Watch Found
A Horse Named Dragon
The Great Detective Race
The Ghost at the Drive-In Movie
The Mystery of the Traveling
  Tomatoes
The Spy Game
The Dog-Gone Mystery
The Vampire Mystery
Superstar Watch
The Spy in the Bleachers
The Amazing Mystery Show
The Clue in the Recycling Bin
Monkey Trouble
The Zombie Project
The Great Turkey Heist
The Garden Thief
The Boardwalk Mystery
The Mystery of the Fallen Treasure
The Return of the Graveyard Ghost
The Mystery of the Stolen Snowboard
The Mystery of the Wild West
  Bandit

For more about the Boxcar Children,
visit them online at

TheBoxcarChildren.com

THE BOXCAR CHILDREN BEGINNING

by Patricia MacLachlan

Before they were the Boxcar Children, Henry, Jessie, Violet, and Benny Alden lived with their parents on Fair Meadow Farm.

978-0-8075-6617-6
US $5.99 paperback

Although times are hard, they're happy—"the best family of all," Mama likes to say. And when a traveling family needs shelter from a winter storm, the Aldens help, and make new friends. But the spring and summer bring events that will change all their lives forever.

Newbery Award–winning author Patricia MacLachlan tells a wonderfully moving story of the Alden children's origins.

* * *

"Fans will enjoy this picture of life 'before.'"—*Publishers Weekly*

"An approachable lead-in that serves to fill in the background both for confirmed fans and readers new to the series." —*Kirkus Reviews*